We're ALL SCREWED!

We're ALL SCREWED!

How Toxic Regulation Will Crush the Free Market System

BY STEPHEN A. BOYKO

PUBLISHING

P.O. Box 849, Cedar Falls, Iowa 50613
www.w-apublishing.com

This book is printed on acid-free paper.

Copyright © 2009 by Stephen A. Boyko. All rights reserved.

Published by W&A Publishing, Cedar Falls, Iowa www.w-apublishing.com.

No part of this book may be reproduced or transmitted in any form or by any means, electronic or mechanical, including photocopying, recording, or by any information storage and retrieval system, except as permitted under Section 107 or 108 of the 1976 United States Copyright Act, without permission in writing from the publisher and the copyright holder. Requests to the publisher for permission should be addressed to P.O. Box 849, Cedar Falls, IA 50613.

In the publication of this book, every effort has been made to offer the most current, correct, and clearly expressed information possible. Nonetheless, inadvertent errors can occur, and rules and regulations governing personal finance and investing often change. Any advice and strategies contained herein may not be suitable for your situation, and there is a risk of loss trading stocks, commodity futures, options, and foreign exchange products. Neither the publisher nor author shall be liable for any loss of profit or any other commercial damages, including but not limited to special, incidental, consequential, or other damages that are incurred as a consequence of the use and application, directly or indirectly, of any information presented in this book. If legal, tax advice, or other expert assistance is required, the services of a professional should be sought.

Library of Congress Control Number: 2009931564
ISBN: 978-1-934354-12-4
ISBN-10: 1-934354-12-0

Printed in the United States of America

10 9 8 7 6 5 4 3 2 1

To Mardena, the story of my life.

CONTENTS

Acknowledgements
vii

Introduction
ix

Part I: Encierro—The Running of the Bulls
1

Part II: Best Practice Governance
43

Part III: Managing Change Results in a Net Benefit
59

Part IV: Effective Governance
95

Part V: Efficient Governance
125

Part VI: A Better Way
159

Glossary
169

Index
181

ACKNOWLEDGEMENTS

This book is the byproduct of 40-plus years of capital market conversations regarding ways to improve the effectiveness and efficiency for investors, issuers, and intermediaries. I am indebted to the patience and engaging minds of three good friends: Merle Coe, Tony Negus, and Brad Smith, who helped establish the intellectual foundation for this text.

I would like to thank W&A Publishing and Russell Wasendorf, Sr., for giving me the opportunity to write *We're All Screwed*, which we all strongly believe to be timely and important to America's economic well being.

Every work of this nature is a team effort that requires coordination of the sequence and timing of ideas. To this end, Heather Larson-Blakestad, executive editor of *SFO Magazine*, provided guidance for the five formative articles; and Karris Golden, executive editor of W&A Publishing, provided invaluable suggestions that kept me focused on the objective and benchmark deadlines.

Special recognition should be given to my family for their encouragement and support—most notably my wife, my first-line editor.

Finally, at the risk of unintentionally omitting someone, I need to thank Steve Anthony; Robert Barbera; Earl F. Burkholder; Phillip Borish; Don Bosic; Bill Carney; Bill Benton; Tom Dourian; Geof Elkind; Mike Falk; Tom Goldsmith; Karen Goober; Aron Gottesman; Nikolas Gvosdev; Shane Massey; James Olson; Geno Jewett; Paul Rose; Allan Sorensen; Peter Stefanou; Taffy Williams; Tony Thien; and Tom Young for reading many chapters, articles, and concept works.

INTRODUCTION

The U.S. capital market is at the most critical juncture in its history. While it is not yet broken, the capital market is in dire need of repair.

The decisions made in the next few months and years will have serious consequences—not just for the "hoped for" economic recovery of the United States, but also for its ability to stay competitive globally further into the future.

Steve and I have spent the majority of our working lives developing and governing capital markets. He is a rational voice with a unique perspective in this debate. In *We're All Screwed: How Toxic Regulation Will Crush the Free Market System*, Steve provides a financial and operational analysis as to what needs to take place in order for governance to be both effective and efficient.

The book does not propose more regulation just for the sake of addressing past deficiencies, but offers an innovative and viable way forward to truly transformative reform. He develops his idea for a new, dynamic three-dimensional approach to regulating, based on segmenting market randomness into predictable, probable, and uncertain governance regimes.

These ideas are amplified with historical references garnered from more than 40 years of capital market experience. It is an innovative, informative, and timely read. Regulators and politicians would do well to heed the principles of governance Steve identifies and bring regulation into the 21st century.

Donald H. Bosic retired from NASDAQ as senior vice president, Corporate Client Group. He has 25 years experience regulating broker-dealers and public companies. As head of NASDAQ Listing Qualifications, he was responsible for monitoring initial and continuing compliance for more than 4,000 NASDAQ-listed companies. He was directly responsible for developing and integrating qualitative and quantitative standards for all NASDAQ companies. Mr. Bosic also developed and managed NASDAQ MarketSite, NASDAQonline.com, and nasdaq.com brand extensions. Prior to his tenure with NASDAQ, he worked for the NASD Inc. (now FINRA), where he managed a professional staff responsible for the regulation of broker-dealers. He later managed the national overview function for regulatory operations and internal department processes. Mr. Bosic now serves as a managing director for Teton Sands Group, a consulting firm.

PART ONE
Encierro — The Running of the Bulls

DON'T CONFUSE BRAINS WITH A BULL MARKET

Much has been written about the calamitous conditions in the capital market brought about by the subprime stock market crash during fall 2008. Critics contend that the governance system of the United States capital market is in disrepair. These same critics question whether it remains the most effective and efficient way to provide capital for American industry.

This section examines the status of the capital market from the perspective of the 34-year bull market. As illustrated by **Wealth Expansion, Dow Jones from 1974 to 2009**, and **Noteworthy Events**, lower Manhattan's financial district in New York City could have been called Pamplona West,[1] as the most famous running of

Wealth Expansion

CATEGORY	1974	1999	CIRCA 2008
Societal ownership	10%	27%	30.3% (05)[2]
NYSE listings	1,935	3,025	6,400 (8/08)[3]
NYSE capitalization	$511 billion	$12 trillion	$26.7 Trillion[4]
NYSE daily volume	$12 million	$700 million	$2.8 billion
Mutual funds	305 funds	6,778 funds	8,015 (01/07)[5]
Capitalization	$56 billion	$4.5 trillion	$12.4 trillion

the bulls was a 34-year financial marathon fueled by capitalism's animal instincts. Those of us who were lucky enough to be investors during this period we should be thankful. We should also be humble, and not confuse brains with a bull mar-

---

[1] The Running of the Bulls (in Spanish *encierro*, from the verb *encerrar*, "to pen"), a nine-day festival of San Fermin in Pamplona, Spain, involves running in front of bulls that have been let loose on a course of sectioned-off town's streets.
[2] U.S. Census for Household Ownership of Equities, 2005.
[3] New York Stock Exchange (NYSE).
[4] As of December 31, 2007, the NYSE had 2,297 listed companies with a combined market capitalization of $15.7 trillion. It is the world's largest stock exchange, both by market capitalization and value of shares traded.
[5] Investment Company Institute (ICI).

Dow Jones Industrial Average Closing Prices, 1974 to 2009

ket. For those in the financial industry at that time it was quite a ride, representing a historical creation of wealth to an expanding group of participants.

It is said that a picture is worth a thousand words. **Wealth Expansion** shows the 34-year record of wealth creation. It is supported by the table on page 4, which identifies the noteworthy events of the Dow Jones Industrial Average (DJIA) from December 6, 1974, to April 30, 2009.

But what I find most interesting is the percentage growth in societal participation in the stock market from approximately 10% in 1974 to 30.3% in 2005, as shown in **Wealth Expansion**.

Granted, there is a certain amount of noise in this statistic—such as differentiating between common stock and preferred stock from mutual funds and whether to include retirement accounts, such as IRAs and pension plan participation. But to the extent possible, societal participation reflects capital market affirmative action, as represented in the Society for International Affairs fact book and U.S. Census Bureau statistics. Of interest are not the statistical differentiations. Instead, the key piece is the social ramification of the increase in societal participation in the capital market.

NETWORK TIPPING POINT

The increase of societal participation suggests that the capital market evolved from a niche market, where the majority of transactions were "sold," to a mass market, where the majority of transactions were "bought."

Noteworthy Events on the DJIA, 1974 to 2009

DATE	DJIA	EVENT
December 6, 1974	577	The last Bear Market bottom
July 12, 1976	1011	Highest point between Jan '73 and Oct. '82
August 12, 1982	776	The start of the "Reagan Bull"
August 25, 1987	2722	The 1987 high
October 19, 1987	1738	The (508 point) crash of 1987
February 2, 1994	3975	The top of the post 1987 crash recovery
November 23, 1994	3674	The start of the Clinton "super bull"
March 29, 1999	10006	The first Dow close above 10000
January 14, 2000	11723	The "Clinton bull" high
March 17, 2000	10630	The biggest one day gain (499 points)
March 20, 2001	9720	Dow closes below previous year low - first time since 1982
Sept 11-14, 2001	9605	Terrorist attack - Dow closed for four days
Sept 17, 2001	8920	The biggest one day fall (685 points)
Sept. 21, 2001	8235	Dow's second worst week ever -14.26%
Dec 31, 2001	10021	Dow up 21.7% from Sept. 21 low but down 7.2% on the year
July 23, 2002	7702	Low close of break below post 9/11 low.
Sept 30, 2002	7591	New 2002 low - All treasury yields (except 30-year bond) at 2002 lows.
Oct 9, 2002	7286	New 2002 low - Dow down 37.8% from Jan 14, 2000 all time high.
Oct 31, 2002	8397	Dow up 806 points (10.6%) for Oct. First "up" month since March.
Nov 6, 2002	8771	Fed cuts rates for first time since Dec. 2001 - 0.50% - Fed Funds 1.25% - Discount 0.75%
Dec 31, 2002	8341	Dow down 16.8% for 2002. First three consecutive year loss since 1939-41
May 23, 2003	8601	Senate passes bill raising the Treasury debt limit by $US 984 Billion to $US 7.384 TRILLION
June 25, 2003	9011	Fed cuts rates by 0.25% to a post 1958 low of 1.00%
Dec 31, 2003	10453	Dow up 25.32% in 2003 - Dollar down 14.67% in 2003
October 3, 2006	11727	Dow exceeds its January 14, 2000 high of 11723
October 9, 2007	14164	New all time high on the Dow
July 2, 2008	11215	Dow closes more than 20% below its Oct. 2007 high - bear market
February 27, 2009	7062	Dow closes at post 1997 low - more than 50% below its Oct. 2007 high.

The growth in online trading illustrates this trend. The United States has the world's most developed online market and has captured substantial market share. As of December 2000, there were 19.3 million online investor accounts, and 894,700 online equity trades were made per day. In 2001, roughly 22% of retail investors traded online.[6]

But even more important is the consequence of the structural increase in societal ownership. If we treat the practitioner (investor, intermediary, and issuer) market activities of researching, pricing, transacting, clearing, settling, and inventorying, etc., as a social network, then a significant insight can be made.

In its simplest form, a social financial network is a map of all of the relevant ties between the nodes of the capital market. Social network analysis views relationships in terms of nodes and ties. Nodes are the individual actors within the networks, and ties are the relationships between the participants. The resulting networks are often quite intricate.

Accordingly, Complexity Theory[7] can help determine the way problems are solved, organizations are run, and the degree to which individuals succeed in achieving their goals within a social financial network. By extension, the growth of societal investor participation can be viewed as a transition from a "Sarnoff" to a "Metcalfe" network.

David Sarnoff was born in Uzlian, Russia, in 1891. He was a pioneer in mass communication and is listed by *Time Magazine*[8] as one of its 100 titans of industry. Sarnoff foresaw radio as a mass medium around which to build a network. He eventually did the same for television.

So it is nearly impossible to imagine that it was 1939 when David Sarnoff told a crowd of curious first-time television viewers, "Now we add sight to sound." His pursuit of a technological comparative advantage turned his employer, Radio Corporation of America (RCA), into a powerhouse in less than a decade. Sarnoff

---

[6] *Online Trading in the United States*, CSU-Research & Policy, HKEx, 2002.
[7] The study of multifaceted systems that brings a new approach to scientific questions that do not fit the usual mechanistic view of reality present in science. In these endeavors, scientists often seek simple, nonlinear coupling rules that lead to complex phenomena, but this need not be the case. Human societies are complex systems in which neither the components nor the couplings are simple. Nevertheless, they exhibit many of the hallmarks of complex systems.
[8] "Builders & Titans," Marcy Carsey and Tom Werner, *Time Magazine*, December 7, 1998.

theorized that the value of a communication network was equal to the number of listeners/viewers.

As a result, Sarnoff's model provides a linear valuation that is consistent with his historical context for one-way communication in radio and television.

Robert Metcalfe was born April 7, 1946, in Brooklyn, New York. He is an electrical engineer who co-invented the Ethernet; founded 3Com, which provides secure network solutions; and formulated Metcalfe's law.

The Ethernet is a family of computer networking technologies for local area networks (LANs).[9] The name comes from the physical concept of ether and is meant to describe the wiring and signaling standards for network models. Metcalfe's law states that the value of a telecommunications network is proportional to the number of connected users in the system. Thus, it describes the possibilities created by Ethernet networks. Metcalfe adds to Sarnoff's law by including communication that goes beyond one-to-many to one-to-one—*in networks of many.*

Illustrative of these kinds of connections are email networks. In such networks, the ability to access anyone in the network adds value to access—even if you do not actually contact every person in the network. Metcalfe's law helps us understand how social networks start as linear functions and then grow exponentially when they reach a critical stage of adoption.[10]

The important point is not to become ensnared in mathematical nuances but to understand that at some time during the 34-year bull market, the social network of investors crossed the 15% population threshold requirement. This caused a linear Sarnoff valuation function to become an exponential Metcalfe valuation function—effecting a shift from "one-to-many" to "one-to-one to many networks." Similar to "adding sight to sound," adding scalability to create exponential financial value forever changed the capital market.

---

[9] Cisco Internetworking Technology Handbook.
[10] "Sarnoff, Metcalf, and Reed: The Secrets to Social Network Growth," Ubernoggin, September 14, 2007. There are other recognized, nonlinear metrics for network valuations: Reed's law, which is somewhat more aggressive than Metcalfe's law; and Zipf's law, which is somewhat more conservative than the valuation provided by Metcalfe's law.

YOU CAN'T PUT HUMPTY TOGETHER AGAIN

From 1933, when the Great Depression-era bank failures subsided, until the Herstatt Bank failure in 1974, there were few financial crises, stock market crashes, or bank failures that were perceived as systemic threats.

Much of this was attributed to the wisdom embodied in the Glass-Steagall Act (GSA). Fundamental to an understanding of the passage of GSA was the severity of the depression in 1933. A quarter of the U.S. working population was unemployed. The nation's banking system was in chaos. More than 11,000 banks had failed or had to merge, reducing the number by 44%, from 25,000 to 14,000.

In point of fact, however, GSA did not change the most important weakness of the Depression-era American banking system: unit banking within states and the prohibition of nationwide banking. This structural flaw is widely considered the principal reason for the failure of so many U.S. banks, where 90% were unit banks with less than $2 million in assets. In contrast, Canada, which had nationwide banking, suffered no bank failures.

GSA's noteworthy accomplishments were the Federal Deposit Insurance Corporation (FDIC) and banking reforms that were designed, in part, to control margin speculation. Some provisions—such as Regulation Q, which allowed the Federal Reserve to regulate interest rates in savings accounts—were later repealed by the Depository Institutions Deregulation and Monetary Control Act of 1980. Prohibitions that prevented bank holding companies from owning other financial companies also were repealed on November 12, 1999, by the Gramm-Leach-Bliley Act. This legislation superseded much of GSA.

The question that needs to be asked in response to any calls for new regulation and systemic market reform is whether GSA was casual, contributory, or coincidental to the remediation of financial services. That is, what role did GSA play in diversifying the financial social network?

Renewed calls for GSA-type governance—as argued and hoped for by a diverse group of policy commentators—are understandable given the level of uncertainty and anxiety associated with the subprime and housing crises in 2008 and 2009. But just as the rooster supposedly raises the sun each morning, is GSA given undeserved credit?

GSA supporters attempt to make the counterfactual argument: What might have happened if GSA had not been repealed? We will never know. The world changed, and different pathways were established to accommodate those changes. It is incorrect to assume GSA could have dealt with market occurrences without difficulty.

Further, while all this sounds soothing and may wrap investors in happy gauze, you cannot put Humpty Dumpty back together again. The investor pathways have evolved into a Metcalfe network. There are global investors with new, innovative products. This has forever altered the nature of the financial services industry; we can't go back to the good old days.

THE COST OF CRASHES AND CRISES

Now we turn to the downside. You will note crises and crashes take much more space to describe. This is analogous to more being written about airplane crashes than safe landings. Although the terms **crisis** and **crash** are treated synonymously in much financial literature, we will differentiate the two for our purposes.

A stock market crash is a sudden, dramatic, double-digit decline in stock prices. Crashes result in a broad-based decline measured across a significant section of a stock market.

In addition, crashes have a consistent pattern that is quite apart from the ebb and flow of the business cycle, argues economist Charles P. Kindleberger,[11] author of *Manias, Panics, and Crashes: A History of Financial Crises*.

Although the terms "crisis" and "crash" are treated synonymously in much of financial literature, we will differentiate the two for our purposes.

Crises are issue specific to a particular event or institution. For example, Bernie Madoff's Ponzi scheme[12] is considered a crisis; if you were not a client of the firm, there is little likelihood of contagion. Conversely, the 2008 subprime bubble is a **crash** because virtually every U.S. citizen is somehow affected.

---

[11] Kindleberger, Charles P., and Robert Aliber. *Manias, Panics and Crashes: A History of Financial Crises*, Fifth Edition, (Wiley Investment Classics, New York, N.Y., 2005) p. 1-22

[12] A fraudulent investment operation that pays returns to investors from their own money or from money paid by subsequent investors rather than from any actual profit earned. The scheme usually offers returns that other investments cannot guarantee, in the form of short-term returns that are abnormally high or unusually consistent. The perpetuation of the returns that a Ponzi scheme advertises and pays requires an ever-increasing flow of money from investors.

However, each group is not without its fuzzy attractors,[13] which can be descriptively profiled to form a group. Common to crises is that they involved pedigrees of the privileged who wanted to become more privileged. No handguns and hoodies here. Crises are perpetrated by the "dress for success crowd" and go after your net worth, not the cash in your wallet.

Banker Iwan Herstatt was born into Cologne, Germany's financial society. Successful Wall Streeters and Nobel Prize winners founded the hedge fund Long-Term Capital Management. Enron, an energy-trading company, was run by prosperous people who graduated from prestigious business schools and had ties to the George W. Bush Administration. Bernard Madoff was a major figure in the National Association of Securities Dealers Automated Quotations (NASDAQ) market as well as a prominent New York City socialite and philanthropist.[14] All were responsible for crises.

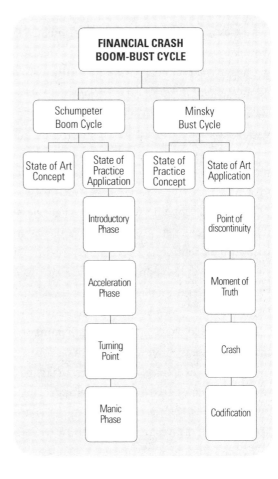

---

[13] From Complexity Theory, it explains the formation of proverbial "dust bunnies" under the bed. Concerned with the long-term behavior of certain kinds of complex systems. Under certain conditions, the systems of interest perform in regular, predictable ways (geometric self-similar shapes, like snowflakes). Under other conditions, the systems exhibit behavior in which regularity and predictability are lost (e.g., bark on trees or lava flows). Almost undetectable differences in initial conditions lead to gradually diverging system reactions until eventually the evolution of behavior is quite dissimilar. The most graphic example of this is the oft-quoted assertion that the flapping of a butterfly's wing can in due course decisively affect weather on a global scale.

[14] "Life Inside the Weird World of Bernard Madoff," Joe Lauria, *Timesonline*, March 22, 2009; and "Who is Bernard Madoff?" Rosie Lavan, *The Times*, December 15, 2008

Stock market crashes are social phenomena where external economic events combine with crowd behavior to form speculative, boom-bust bubbles, as diagramed in the **Financial Crash Boom-Bust Cycle** schematic[15] on page 9. The boom segment integrates state-of-practice (SOP) technologies or products with state-of-art (SOA) applications. This integration changes the terms of competitive engagement and creates profit opportunities for early adapters.

In essence, existing products or techniques are creatively applied to a new purpose. For example, SOP government communication bulletin board was put to SOA commercial use and *voila*—the Internet was born.

Each cycle contains **four phases**. The boom's cycle **introductory phase** finds the demand for a new product application and its assumptions to be of maximum impact. This reinforces a need to reconfigure existing technologies for proof of concept to meet new opportunities.

The **acceleration phase** produces the ability to do something you always wanted to do—if only you had thought of it.

The critical phase is the **inflection point** of the boom cycle, as the rise in the rate of increase is about to go hyperbolic.

In the **manic phase**, a new reality makes it seem as if all things are possible. Investors buy high in the hopes of selling higher. They jettison cash for less-liquid asset categories, such as speculative stocks, commodities, etc. It is the capital market equivalent of **Gresham's law**.[16] **Noise traders**[17] seek to become rich without a real understanding of the processes involved.

The bust segment finds SOA technology being introduced. To fund the development of next-generation technology and capture market share from SOP practitioners, a robust story of extreme optimism is told. Financial *pro forma* make use of long-term extrapolations of the manic phase's short-term hyperbolic growth. This creates an unstable, far-from-equilibrium condition. Further, much of the funding of growth is usually in the form of debt (*Why dilute equity in the 'golden goose'?*), which adds to the instability of the trend.

---

[15] This boom-bust schematic draws models put forth by Charles P. Kindleberger and George Soros.
[16] Bad money drives good money out of circulation as people hoard the valued currency.
[17] Describes an investor who makes trading decisions without the use of fundamental data. These investors generally have poor timing, follow trends, and overreact to good and bad news. The concept is hotly debated in behavioral finance, as many investors believe they are not noise traders and therefore only make well-informed investment decisions.

Similarly, the bust cycle has four phases. The **point of discontinuity** is the inflection point of the bust cycle, where the adjustment in the rate of change turns negative. A divergence between reality and the new application's presumed benefit is recognized. The "moment of truth" occurs when profits narrow, as high-cost SOA technological innovations are sought to achieve original forecasts.

The "bust" creates a reduction of expenditure due to overcapacity. Sharp stock-price declines happen quickly. This phase becomes a self-feeding panic as the bubble bursts. Investors take greater and greater losses to meet loan calls. A *de facto* credit rationing takes place, as bank balance sheets become more important than their income statements.

It is a perverse form of adverse selection, where cash becomes king.[18] The **codification phase** finds market demand is satisfied at a replacement rate. Weak competitors consolidate through mergers and acquisitions. What was SOA technology becomes a commodity, and the process is repeated. Societal codifications, such as laws and taxes, remedy the previous trend's biases and abuses.

ANALYZING CRASHES USING VARIOUS ECONOMIC SCHOOLS OF THOUGHT

Stock market crashes are different and distinct from systemic economic problems like depressions and recessions. A three-by-three matrix juxtaposes conceptual constructs of market efficiency and informational symmetry to compare and contrast the Classical, Monetarian, Neoclassical Keynesian, and Post-Keynesian/ Schumpeterian schools of economic thought.

Information and market performance form the essence of market analysis. Material information is that which would likely affect a stock's price once it becomes known to informed and rational investors. Asymmetrical information results when the party initiating the transaction has better information than the counter-party creating a comparative competitive advantage. For example, the seller of a used car usually has more specific knowledge than the buyer.

---

[18] Kindleberger, Charles P., and Robert Aliber. *Manias, Panics and Crashes: A History of Financial Crises*, Fifth Edition, (Wiley Investment Classics, New York, N.Y., 2005) p. 24-38.

Competing Ideologies Offer Different Approaches

INFORMATION / MARKET	SYMMETRICAL	ASYMMETRICAL
Efficient	Monetarists	Asymmetrical information framework
Inefficient	Neoclassical Keynesians	Post-Keynesians

I argue here and elsewhere in the text that asymmetrical information is an unintended consequence of poorly structured governance regimes. Economic fundamentalism supports one-size-fits-all regulatory regimes and frustrates the natural tendency of markets to segment as they mature.

Market evolution separates information into predictable (U.S. Treasury), probabilistic (large-cap, S&P100 issuers), and uncertain (small-cap, negative cash-flow issuers) regimes based on the underlying economic environment's degree of randomness. Markets self-select efficient development pathways to minimize a group's or market externality's competitive advantage due to "local knowledge."

For example, *scienter* is a legal term that refers to intent or knowledge of wrongdoing. This means that an offending party has knowledge of the "wrongness" of an act or event prior to committing it. If you unknowingly sell a car with brakes that do not work, your actions do not constitute *scienter*. If you sell the car and know of the problem prior to the sale, you have *scienter*.[19]

It also is important to considered the buyer's perspective, because consumer rights must be proportionate to consumer responsibilities to lessen free riding and moral hazard. Transparent disclosure regarding counter-party's interests changes the buyer's level due diligence.

So if the seller is a new car salesperson from a recognized dealership, that is a case of **predictability**; a used car salesperson from a recognized dealership, **probability**; or an individual selling a car on his front lawn, **uncertainty**.

My correspondence with Ohio State University law professor Paul Rose augments this point:

---

[19] West's Encyclopedia of American Law (Thomson Gale, New York, N.Y.)

"It is still too easy to sue companies based on information that, with a hindsight bias, turns out not to have come about the way management said it would. Those plaintiffs almost never win at trial, though, unless the plaintiffs can show that the managers knowingly lied about what their beliefs were. In other words, if I make a prediction that turns out to be incorrect, most courts would only hold me liable if the plaintiffs could show that I didn't believe my own prediction (an almost impossible task, given that discovery is delayed until after plaintiffs win against my motion to dismiss). They would not win if my prediction did not turn out to be correct, though, so long as I stayed within the safe harbors granted by the courts, SEC rules, and the PSLRA[20] (essentially, these safe harbors require identifying information that is forward-looking, and acknowledging that it may turn out to not come true). In the end, I don't think that the doctrine of scienter works against your system [randomness, segmentation], but largely aligns with it." [21]

Professor Eugene Fama of the University of Chicago Booth School of Business developed the efficient-market hypothesis (EMH) in the early 1960s for his doctoral dissertation. He defines an **efficient** market as one that has large numbers of rational profit maximizers. These investors actively compete with each other, trying to predict future market prices. Competition means the full effects of new information are reflected instantaneously.[22]

Crashes cause problems for efficient market advocates, Classical economists, and Monetarists. It is difficult for them to imagine an efficient market lacking information that could cause a sudden 20% drop in prices.

---

[20] *The United States Private Securities Litigation Reform Act of 1995*, Pub. L. 104-67, 109 Stat. 737 (codified as amended in 15 sections of U.S. Code). PSLRA implemented several substantive changes affecting certain cases brought under the federal securities laws, including changes related to pleading, discovery, liability, class representation, and awards fees and expenses. It was designed to reduce the number of frivolous securities lawsuits filed in federal courts. The act states that investors cannot proceed with a case unless they already have evidence of a deliberate fraud. Prior to PSLRA, a case could proceed with minimal evidence and use pretrial discovery to search for more. Now, plaintiffs must begin with such evidence.
[21] From Boyko's correspondence with Rose.
[22] Fama, Eugene. *Financial Analysts Journal*, 1965.

Further, my Wall Street experience gives me pause in supporting the concept of "informed, rational investors." I have discovered that many investors are better at *rationalizing* than *analyzing*. Their inclination is to protect themselves from the calamitous decisions that cause investment depletion, not necessarily to develop informed, rational investment assessments.

Many investors tend to hear what they want to hear. So if there is static in the message, is it due to trouble with the transmitter (the market) or receiving antenna (the investor's ability to process information)?

Beginning with Classical Economics, let's investigate the schools of economic thought for guidance as to the prediction, management, and possible prevention of stock market crashes.

Classical economists favor free trade and laissez-faire or "hands off" governance. The Classical school of economic theory began with the 1776 publication of Adam Smith's monumental work, *The Wealth of Nations*. The book identified land, labor, and capital as the three factors of production and the major contributors to a nation's wealth.

In Smith's view, the ideal economy is a dynamic, self-regulating system that automatically satisfies the economic needs of the populace. He described the market mechanism as an "invisible hand" that leads all individuals—in pursuit of their own self-interests—to produce the greatest benefit for society as a whole.[23]

Smith's views are balanced with the philosophies Jean-Baptiste Say, best known for saying, "Supply creates its own demand." Say's Law of Markets embodied the unstated suggestion that all payments for goods are immediately spent on other goods. That postulate reflected the belief that money plays no part in the functioning of the economy (beyond its role as a medium of exchange) because it would be irrational to acquire and simply save money, thereby forfeiting the benefits of consumption or investment.[24] All goods supplied are consumed at equilibrium.

Monetarism is an economic school of thought that stresses the primary importance of money supply in determining nominal Gross Domestic Product (GDP) and price level. Founded upon Classical assumptions of market efficiency,

---

[23] *Major Schools of Economic Theory*, Education Resources, Federal Reserve Bank of San Francisco.
[24] Say, Jean Baptiste, translated by C.R. Prinsep. M.A., *A Treatise on Political Economy or The Production, Distribution, and Consumption of Wealth* (Scholarly Publishing Office, University of Michigan Library, Ann Arbor, Michigan, 2005) p. 61-90.

Monetarism confronts asymmetrical information from mixed governmental monetary policy signals. Monetarists advocate rational expectations, holding that government attempts to control the economy are doomed because economic actors, such as Enron, could easily game the outcome.[25]

Inefficient public policy can reduce commercially viable industries to minimalist levels of self-sustainability. Reference the California electricity crisis of 2000 and 2001, where utilities agreed to have their rates capped at levels once considered commercially viable. Notwithstanding above-average population growth, California restricted building electric utility infrastructure and transmission distribution systems, which severely constrained new generating capacity. When utilities could not pass on to their customers the cost of electricity without exceeding the original caps, the result was power shortages, bankruptcies, and excess rates.

Further, California confused "firm" with "market" governance structures. Unlike natural gas or petroleum, electricity cannot be inventoried. If there are infrastructure enhancement issues and no inventories, chances are the governance structure is for a market, not a firm. Imposing firm remedies on market maladies resulted in the economic equivalent of pouring gasoline on a fire, enabling energy companies, such as Enron and Reliant Energy, to take advantage of the system.

If a stockbroker has an elderly investor seeking income and recommends a speculative security with no dividend, that stockbroker is censured and fined. Conversely, when the *nomenklatura*[26] (whether *apparatchiks*[27] or regulators) are permitted to appropriate capital surpluses (shareholder dividends) with impunity to subsidize sub-optimal policy, this conversion of private capital to cover unsatisfactory performance is called "progressive." Bad governance begets bad regulation, which begets bad results.

Monetarism, on the other hand, tries to simplify the governance process to minimize regulatory inefficiencies. It is a mixture of theoretical ideas, philosophical beliefs, and policy prescriptions based on:

---

[25] Barbera, Robert, *The Cost of Capitalism*, (McGraw-Hill, New York, N.Y., 2009) p. 167.
[26] An elite group or class from which candidates and appointees for top-level positions are selected, especially in politics.
[27] A derogatory term for an official who is part of a large organization or political party.

1. The theoretical foundation of the Quantity Theory of Money.[28]
2. The belief that markets are efficient and work best when left alone. Laissez-faire is usually the best practice. Fiscal policy is often conflicted.
3. The guiding policy that the Federal Reserve System should have a fixed monetary policy. It is only during market crashes that the central bank should function as the lender of last resort to prevent a financial problem from becoming an economic problem.

The "Founding Father of Monetarism" is economist Milton Friedman.[29] Inflation was high and rising throughout the 1970s, and Friedman convincingly attributed this to rapid increases in the money supply. He argued that the economy may be complicated, but monetary policy does not have to be. When there is a short supply of money there will be upward pressure on interest rates, and vice versa.

The key to good policy is to control the supply of money, which Monetarists believe to be the most effective and efficient way to limit boom-bust perturbations.

Keynesians adhere to philosophies set forth by John Maynard Keynes' *General Theory of Employment, Interest and Money.* published in 1936, the book advocated government spending to increase aggregate demand. Keynes denies Smith's invisible hand. This was a major departure from Classical Economics and Say's Law. Keynesians evolved into two groups: **Neoclassical Keynesians** and **Post-Keynesians**.[30]

Neoclassical Keynesians are influenced by Nobel Laureate Joseph Stiglitz.[31] They take their insights from Keynes and combine it in the general framework of Classical Economics. This school of thought is the economics of imperfection—price inflexibility, informational asymmetries, and the like.

---

[28] The equation of exchange is the building block for monetarist theory. It states that $M \times V = P \times Y$, where M is the quantity of M1; V is velocity of M1; or the average number of times that the dollar turns over in a given year on the purchase of final goods and services; P is the price level; and Y is real output.

[29] Friedman (1923-3006), an American economist at the University of Chicago and the Hoover Institute, influenced the economic policies of several U.S. presidents. He was awarded the 1976 Nobel Prize in Economics for achievements in the fields of consumption analysis, monetary history and theory, and demonstration of the complexity of stabilization policy.

[30] Barbera, Robert, *The Cost of Capitalism*, (McGraw-Hill, New York, N.Y., 2009) p. 164

[31] Joseph Eugene Stiglitz (born 1943), an American economist and professor at Columbia University in New York City, received the John Bates Clark Medal (1979) and the 2001 Nobel Memorial Prize in Economics. He also is the former senior vice president and chief economist of the World Bank.

Yet because all are equally burdened, there is symmetry. Economists adapt and innovate to overcome the inefficiencies of the marketplace. Like the Beijing butterfly whose flapping wings create a tornado in Kansas, every so often a mutation trying to adapt to the uncertainty of imperfection causes markets to crash.

Neoclassical Keynesians are differentiated from Post-Keynesians by their perspectives on capital investment information. This is the cornerstone of macroeconomic dynamics. It raises the question of whether or not the agents involved in the investment decision have the information needed to make optimal choices—individually and collectively—which is central to capital accumulation theory. New Classical and Neoclassical Keynesian theories assume they do. Keynesian and Post-Keynesian theories assume they do not.[32]

As Professor James Crotty of the University of Massachusetts frames the issue, "Confronting the theory of agent choice is: What do the agents know about the future, and how do they come to know it?"

Can economists evolve data to information to knowledge? Do they have this type of predictive capability? Can they model market realities? I believe they can for predictable and probabilistic underlying economic environments, but not for *uncertain economic environments*. This error of omission—the failure to disclose indeterminism,[33] created much of the subprime problem.

Economists of Change are **Schumpeterians** and **Post-Keynesians**. They are the economic drivers of the boom-bust cycle.

Schumpeterian entrepreneurs feed the boom cycle through "creative destruction," while the **Minsky Moment** describes the realities of the debt-driven bust cycle.[34]

---

[32] Crotty, James, *Are Keynesian Uncertainty and Macrotheory Compatible? Conventional Decision Making, Institutional Structures, and Conditional Stability in Keynesian Macromodels*, (University of Massachusetts, Amherst, Massachusetts, 1994)

[33] Based on the idea that because people have free will, their actions cannot always be accurately predicted by past behavior and events.

[34] Barbera, Robert, *The Cost of Capitalism*, (McGraw-Hill, New York, N.Y., 2009) p. 170-178. H.P. Minsky identified three types of borrowers that contribute to the accumulation of insolvent debt: hedge borrowers; speculative borrowers; and Ponzi borrowers. The hedge borrower makes debt payments (covering interest and principal) from current cash flows from investments. Speculative borrowers use cash flow from investments to service the debt, but must regularly roll over the principal. Ponzi borrowers believe the appreciation of the value of the asset will be sufficient to refinance the debt but cannot make sufficient payments on interest or principal with the cash flow from investments.

Schumpeterians see the process of **creative destruction** as the essential economic dynamic. Entrepreneurs perturb Walrasian equilibrium[35] with transformative societal innovations. This in turn forces the adoption of new patterns of production and consumption.

Joseph Schumpeter had little use for the idealizations of "perfect competition" or the reputed rationality of the free market. He ridiculed the notion of market equilibrium and saw little value in market efficiency. Stability was only a relative and temporary condition—a lull in between moments of radical mutation.

Schumpeter is a goose gaggler trying to cultivate an entrepreneurial "black swan."[36] Although considered the godfather of entrepreneurs, Schumpeter preferred monopolies and oligopolies, with their ability to realize economies of scale.[37]

Schumpeter's concern about asymmetrical information was minimized by the function of intermediaries, who enabled entrepreneurs to profit by introducing innovations. He agreed with Minsky's analysis of the role of financial institutions by specifying the conditions that categorized the repayment the loans.[38]

Post-Keynesians are represented by Kindleberger[39] and Hyman Minsky.[40] They argue that much of Keynes' insight was lost in the Neoclassical synthesis, be-

---

[35] An allocation vector pair where X represents the quantities of each good held by each agent and P represents the price for each good. Each agent makes optimal choices commensurate with his or her budget. If an agent prefers another combination of goods, he or she cannot afford it. (Based on the theory developed by French economist Leon Walras.)

[36] Forgive the mixed metaphor; it by design to profile Schumpeter's economic viewpoint. What other right-wing, pro-capitalist economist would value Marx's input?

[37] Schumpeter, Joseph Alois. *Capitalism, Socialism, and Democracy*, (Harper Perennial Modern Classics, New York, N.Y., 2008) p. 45-63.

[38] "The Role of Banks in Financing Small and Medium Firms," Giancarlo Bertocco, *Economics and Quantitative Methods*, No. qf0308, July 2003; Kindleberger, Charles P., and Robert Aliber. *Manias, Panics and Crashes: A History of Financial Crises*, Fifth Edition, (Wiley Investment Classics, New York, N.Y., 2005) p. 27-28.

[39] Charles P. Kindleberger obituary, *The Tech*, Massachusetts Institute of Technology, July 9, 2003. A historical economist, Kindleberger (1910-2003) authored more than 30 books. After 1948, he focused on teaching at MIT. Prior to that, he worked for the Federal Reserve Bank of New York, the Bank of International Settlements in Switzerland, and the Board of Governors of the Federal Reserve System.

[40] "H.P. Minsky, 77, Economist who Decoded Lending Trends," Louis Uchitelle, *New York Times*, October 26, 1996. Minsky (1919-1996), was an American economist and professor of economics at Washington University in St. Louis. His research attempted to provide an understanding and explanation of the characteristics of financial crises. Often described as a post-Keynesian economist, he supported some government intervention in financial markets, opposed some of the popular deregulation policies in the 1980s, and argued against accumulation of debt.

cause of an attempt to preserve too much of the Classical economic context.[41] Unlike their counterparts, Kindleberger and Minsky have a much broader definition of what constitutes a financial crash. They argue that financial crashes involve either sharp decline in asset prices, failures of large financial and non-financial firms, deflations or disinflations, disruptions in foreign exchange markets, or some combination of all of these.

A major problem with the Kindleberger-Minsky view was its lack of rigor in characterizing a financial dislocation. This proved troublesome for the Post-Keynesians, who used too broad a justification for government interventions. Often this was counterproductive and did not benefit the economy.[42]

Frederic Mishkin[43] provided clarification for the Post-Keynesians with a more workable description of financial dislocations. He defined a financial crash[44] as a disruption to markets in which adverse selection and moral hazards impaired the markets' ability to effectively and efficiently allocate resources. The result is a sharp decline in economic output.

The "**Minsky Moment**," a term coined by Paul McCulley of PIMCO,[45] occurs when the growth rate of the debt's carrying cost exceeds the growth rate of the market's real rate of appreciation. Therefore, the Minsky Moment is instructive when trying to understand the market's bursting bubble denouement.

Minsky proposed theories linking financial market fragility in the normal life cycle of an economy with speculative investment bubbles endogenous to financial markets. He claimed that in prosperous times excess corporate cash flow rises beyond what is needed. A speculative euphoria develops. This explains why bubbles go higher and last longer than logic would suggest. At higher prices there are a greater number of intrepid investors who can pyramid speculative profits.

---

[41] Barbera, Robert, *The Cost of Capitalism*, (McGraw-Hill, New York, N.Y., 2009) p. 164.
[42] "Asymmetric Information and Financial Crises: A Historical Perspective," Frederic S. Mishkin, *Financial Markets and Financial Crises*, (University of Chicago Press, Chicago, Illinois, January 1991) p.70.
[43] An American economist, Mishkin (1951) teaches at the Columbia Business School. He also was a member of the Federal Reserve System Board of Governors (2006 to 2008). He has authored several books, and his work emphasizes the impact of monetary policy on financial markets and the aggregate economy.
[44] Quantitatively, a market crash is a price decline of greater than 20% in a short period.
[45] PIMCO is a money management company founded on the philosophy that hard work, high standards, and the desire to be the best are critical to success.

For example, Alan Greenspan was the chair of the Federal Reserve of the United States from 1987 to 2006. From August 1987 to November 2005, the monetary base rose from $233.5 billion to $782.5 billion—a 235% total increase, or 6.8% annually. The M3[46] measure of money supply rose during the same period from $3.62 trillion to more than $100 trillion, a 179% increase, or 5.8% annually.

Greenspan's critics argue that during his tenure as Fed chairman he allowed the growth in the money supply to greatly exceed the global supply of gold's historic growth rate of 1% to 2% per year.[47] This excess liquidity laid the foundation for the subprime bubble.[48]

Policymakers face queries about what they should do to prevent financial crises and crashes. How should they respond when a financial dislocation appears imminent? What are the consequences of their actions?

To understand this, you must first understand the nature of financial crises and crashes and how they might affect the total economy. The following examines four crises and four crashes through the prism of various economic schools of thought.

APPLIED ECONOMICS: REGULATORY REFORM THROUGH INFRASTRUCTURE AND RULE CHANGES

The period following the World War II era until 1974 marked a period of relative calm in the capital markets. Conversely, the period from 1974 to 2009 saw a significant increase in the number and the absolute size of financial crises and stock market crashes. During the latter period, the market loss resulting from crashes

---

[46] *Discontinuance of M3, U.S. Federal Reserve*, revised March 9, 2006. M0 or "monetary base" is notes and coins in circulation and bank vaults and the reserves of commercial banks. M1 is currency outside the U.S. Treasury, Federal Reserve banks, depository vaults, and other checkable deposits. M2 is close substitutes for money and the combination of M1 plus savings deposits, time deposits less than $100,000, and individual money market deposit accounts. M3 is M2 plus large time deposits, institutional money market funds, short-term repurchase agreements, and larger liquid assets. The U.S. central bank no longer publishes/discloses M3 to the public.

[47] "The Mess Alan Greenspan Leaves Behind," Stefan M.I. Karlsson, the Ludwig Von Mises Institute and *Money Week*, June 26, 2006

[48] Greenspan's defenders noted that because the total monetary mass and currency in circulation increased proportionately to one another, total reserves were essentially frozen.

Financial Crashes and Crises

CRISIS	NATURE	TIME FRAME	APPROXIMATE COST / WORKOUT	REGULATORY RESPONSE
Herstatt Bank of Cologne	Crisis	1974	$112 million	CLS and RTGS
Crash of 1987	Crash	1987	$1 trillion	Circuit breakers
S&L debacle	Crash	1989	$153 billion	RTC
Long Term Capital Mgt.	Crisis	1998	$3.6 billion	President's report
Dot-com	Crash	2001	$5 trillion	
Enron	Crisis	2002	$57 billion	Sarbanes-Oxley
Madoff	Crisis	2008	$64.8 billion	SEC Anti-fraud
Subprime	Crash	2008	$8 trillion	FASB 157

increased from $1 trillion for the 1987 stock market crash[49] to a guesstimated $8 trillion for the 2008 subprime crash.[50]

Although much hand-wringing has taken place since 1987, the facts indicate that while financial perturbations are more frequent and larger, the severity of the dislocations has been greatly muted by the push-back from the capital market's annual appreciation rate of approximately 11% (the DJIA was 1738 in 1987 and 14,164 in 2007).

For example, the post-subprime stock market crash rally appreciated more than 30% from the March 2009 lows. Thus, like much financial commentary, analysis of financial crises and market crashes becomes very much the case of whether the analyst wants to focus on the music or the static.

Financial Crashes and Crises (above) references four crashes and four crises. We will review these events and explore their historical significance. We will ana-

---

[49] *Financial Crisis Management: Four Financial Crises in the 1980s*, U.S. General Accounting Office Staff Study, May 1997, p. 60-69. The San Francisco FRB loss estimate was $800 billion.

[50] "How Severe is Subprime Mess?" *Associated Press*, March 13, 2007; "Making Sense of the Mess," Mara Der Hovanesian, Peter Coy, Matthew Goldstein, and David Henry *BusinessWeek*, March 19, 2007; "What History Tells Us About the Market," Jason Zweig, *Wall Street Journal*, October 11, 2008; "Gonna Need a Bigger Boat," Thomas L. Friedman, *New York Times*, November 16, 2008; and "With Assets Less Toxic, U.S. Banks Have Other Woes," Jim Kuhnhenn, *Associated Press*, July 9, 2009. The crash resulted in an estimated $8 trillion loss, given the 50% market decline. As of December 31, 2007, the NYSE had 2,297 listed companies with a combined market capitalization of $15.7 trillion. The total world derivatives market has been estimated at $791 trillion face or nominal value—11 times the size of the entire world economy. The derivatives market value is stated in notional, or hypothetical, values. As a result, we cannot directly compare it to a stock or a fixed-income security, which traditionally refers to an actual value. Moreover, the vast majority of derivatives cancel out each other (i.e., a bet on an event occurring is offset by a comparable bet on the event not occurring). Many such relatively illiquid securities are valued as marked-to-model, not an actual market price. This creates a larger decline than would otherwise have occurred.

lyze the mindset of policymakers by reverse engineering the regulatory response in terms of new rules and infrastructure enhancements from the aftermath of the examined financial crashes and crises.

Between 1974, which brought us the last bear market bottom and the Herstatt Bank currency-driven collapse, and 2008's subprime bubble burst, we find the analytical timeframe for the bust cycle events.

The Herstatt Bank of Cologne, Germany, was a privately owned by Iwan Herstatt. It became insolvent in June 1974 due to foreign exchange speculation. The collapse was, at the time, the largest bank failure in German postwar history.

The Herstatt crisis had "the-check's-in-the-mail" implications for the regulatory framework in terms of settlement risk. **Settlement risk** occurs between the trade execution and settlement, when there is a counter-party default in delivering a security or its value in cash.

Continuous Linked Settlement (CLS) was created in September 2002 by a number of the world's largest banks for the purpose of settling foreign exchange flows amongst themselves. The process known as **Real Time Gross Settlement** (RTGS) is a system in which processing and final settlement of funds transfer instructions take place continuously to minimize asynchronous time lag risks.

Often overlooked in today's capital market is the evolution of back-office capabilities. In the late 1960s and early 1970s, a crunch of back-office paperwork caused Wall Street brokerage problems that nearly bankrupted the NYSE.

Unable to keep up with trades on the NYSE and other exchanges, brokerage firms sustained heavy losses. Volume of 10 million shares per day could not be processed and caused the NYSE to close each Tuesday and Thursday afternoon to process the backlog of trades. The formation of the **National Clearing Corporation**, which immobilized stock certificates through a continuous net settlement process, created the global, robust market that can now settle and clear a volume of two billion shares per day.

Lessons learned: Much like the images and soundtrack for a movie, front-office sales and innovative products are inexorably linked to back-office processing capabilities. If one gets too far removed from the other, asynchronous problems occur.

Merrill Lynch became Merrill Lynch in part because it viewed its back office as a profit center from which to maximize profits, not merely a place to minimize costs efficiently.

By extension, it is easier to get buy-in via incentives. In 1970, this enabled Merrill Lynch to absorb the NYSE's fifth-largest brokerage house, Goodbody &

Company,[51] when the company fell victim to Wall Street's so-called "paper-crunch disaster."[52] Overextended trading houses were generating more transaction records than their accounting departments could process.

For Goodbody and many others, this resulted in massive confusion and eventual collapse. The NYSE asked Merrill Lynch to step in and help Goodbody. Merrill Lynch eventually acquired Goodbody at the end of 1970. The bailout cost little and brought Merrill Lynch new expertise in the area of product development and institutional goodwill.[53]

The 1987 stock market crash began on October 19, when a large and rapid sell-off of equity securities led to mechanical and liquidity problems in trading and financial systems at stock, options, and futures exchanges and associated clearing organizations.

Specialists did not open for trading and traders did not answer their phones; it was complete and utter chaos.

There was a surreal aspect to the crash. Messages came across the intercom announcing that order imbalances had suspended trading in the most liquid of stocks, such as IBM. The power of "The Street" was in the hands of margin clerks as they determined how many shares to liquidate so they could meet the call loans that financed margin trades.

The crash was extraordinary in terms of the speed and extent of falling prices and skyrocketing trading volume. From the close of trading on Tuesday, October 13, to the close of trading on Monday, October 19, the DJIA declined by almost one-third, representing a loss in value of approximately $1 trillion for all outstanding U.S. stocks. On October 19, the DJIA plunged another 508 points (23%[54]). NYSE volume was 604 million shares—more than twice the average daily volume for the year.[55]

But in reality, the October 19, 1987, DJIA of 1738 was the greatest buying opportunity of the last quarter century. Wall Street was hosting a historic sale. For

---

[51] Weiner, Eric J. *What Goes Up: The Uncensored History of Modern Wall Street as Told by the Bankers, Brokers, CEOs, and Scoundrels Who Made it Happen* (Little, Brown and Company, New York, N.Y., 2005) p. 147-148.

[52] Ibid.

[53] *International Directory of Company Histories*, Vol. 13 (St. James Press, 1996).

[54] In excess of the 20% threshold for a crash standard.

[55] *Financial Crisis Management: Four Financial Crises in the 1980s*, U.S. General Accounting Office Staff Study, May 1997, p. 60-69.

the next 20 years, the DJIA would appreciate approximately 11.5%. Given this rate of return, an index fund would double in value every 6.2 years.[56]

Lessons learned: The 1987 market crash resulted in large part from institutional asset-allocators executing pre-programmed, stop-loss sell orders[57] in concert with specific price points for stocks and futures contracts.

The story of the 1831 collapse of the Broughton Bridge near Manchester, England, helps explain the lesson. Bridges have many natural, low frequencies of vibration, so it is possible for a column of soldiers marching in step to vibrate the bridge at one of the its natural frequencies.

The bridge locks onto the frequency while the soldiers' steps continue to add to the alternating motions, causing increasingly larger bridge oscillations, or forward and backward movements.[58]

We can learn from the collapse of the Broughton Bridge: A financial equivalent of the now-standard practice of breaking cadence when soldiers cross a bridge was necessary in 1987. At that time, the asset-allocators' orders caused a financial vibration that almost collapsed the market.

Enter the concept of **circuit breakers**, which the SEC approved on April 15, 1998, in amendments to NYSE Rule 80B (*Trading Halts Due to Extraordinary Market Volatility*). By implementing a pause in trading at specified price points, the market, in essence, breaks cadence. Investors are given time to assimilate incoming information. They then have the ability to make informed choices during periods of high market volatility without falling victim to herd behavior.

Prior to the **Savings & Loan (S&L) crash** of the late 1980s, it was estimated that by the mid-1980s 35% of the country's S&Ls were not profitable. An additional 9% were technically bankrupt.

---

[56] Rule of 72: the idea that there are methods for estimating an investment's doubling time. The number 72 is divided by the interest percentage per period to obtain the approximate number of periods (usually years) required for doubling.

[57] Order placed with an agent to sell a security when it reaches a certain price; designed to limit an investor's loss on a security position.

[58] Carlson, James A., and Jennifer M. Johnson. *Multivariable Mathematics with Maple: Linear Algebra, Vector Calculus and Differential Equations,* (Prentice-Hall, New York, N.Y., 1996) p. 255-260.

As financial institutions went under, state and federal insurance programs began to run out of the money needed to refund depositors. By 1989, Congress agreed on a taxpayer-financed bailout measure known as the Financial Institutions Reform Recovery and Enforcement Act (FIRREA).

The bill was adopted in 1989 and provided $50 billion to close failed banks and stop further losses. It set up a new government agency called the Resolution Trust Corporation (RTC) to resell S&L assets, and use the proceeds to pay back depositors. FIRREA also changed S&L regulations to help improve price-discovery investment guidelines for loan originations.

Between 1986 and 1995, more than 1,000 banks with total assets greater than $500 billion failed. By 1999, the crash cost $153 billion, with taxpayers footing $124 billion of that bill and the S&L industry paying the rest.[59]

If it were not for the experience with the RTC precedent, it doubtful the U.S. Department of The Treasury could have implemented the Troubled Asset Relief Program (TARP) as quickly as it did in the aftermath of the 2008 subprime crash.

The S&L experience yielded three important lessons:[60]

- Excessive regulation was the initial cause of the industry's problems. The rates S&Ls paid depositors were controlled. Those interest-rate ceilings were designed to protect S&Ls from high funding costs. Caught in a squeeze between stagnant incomes and rising costs, the S&L industry's capital eroded. By 1980, before any deregulation had taken place, the liabilities of the S&L industry exceeded its assets by $110 billion. The industry was already insolvent when Congress and the James Carter Administration enacted the Depository Institutions Deregulation and Monetary Control Act of 1980.[61]
- Federal deposit insurance was ultimately responsible for the high costs of the debacle. George Kaufman, John F. Smith Professor of Finance and Economics at Loyola University in Chicago, observed, "Deregulation is only effective in increasing efficiency if the reduction in government

---

[59] "What was the Savings & Loan Crisis?" Kimberly Amadeo, About.com.
[60] "Lessons from the Savings & Loan Debacle: The Case for Further Financial Deregulation," Catherine England, *Regulation: The Cato Review of Business & Government*, Summer 1992.
[61] "Lessons from the Savings & Loan Debacle: The Case for Further Financial Deregulation," Catherine England, *Regulation: The Cato Review of Business & Government*, Summer 1992.

discipline is replaced by a compensating increase in market discipline." For insolvent S&Ls during the 1980s, there was no market discipline. Neither owners nor depositors had anything to lose, which resulted in both groups feeling encouraged to escalate in their risk-taking. Federally insured depositors were largely unconcerned with the health of the institutions in which they placed money. Undercapitalized S&Ls could assure themselves a continuing influx of funds by simply offering to pay slightly higher interest rates than their competitors. Unlike other industries, where failing firms find their funding dries up no matter what price they offer; insolvent S&Ls faced no such constraints. The 1980s were, in fact, marked by perverse runs in which funds flowed from stronger banks and S&Ls to the weakest depositories. For S&Ls, federal deposit insurance short-circuited the market's natural risk-braking mechanisms.[62]

- Finally, government-sponsored efforts to protect the industry only invited abuses and increased the ultimate cost of restructuring. The S&L crisis was a mishandled industry-restructuring problem. When the government becomes committed to protecting and subsidizing a particular industry for "the social good," policymakers are often tempted to ignore and even override market signals that indicate the true nature of the continued utility of that industry. Such efforts are rarely successful. Forbearance[63] was rationalized by the supposed disruption to be caused by the forced closing of hundreds of S&Ls. In the end they were closed anyway. For all the government's efforts, reduction of the industry proceeded. In 1979 there were 4,500 S&Ls; in 1991 about 2,200 S&Ls remained. Meanwhile, delaying tactics, which were designed to protect *industry members*, cost *taxpayers* and other financial market participants hundreds of billions of dollars.[64]

---

[62] "Lessons from the Savings & Loan Debacle: The Case for Further Financial Deregulation," Catherine England, *Regulation: The Cato Review of Business & Government*, Summer 1992.

[63] A special agreement between the mortgage lender and borrower to delay a foreclosure. Borrowers sometimes have problems making payments, prompting the lender to begin foreclosure. To avoid foreclosure, the lender and borrower can make a forbearance agreement, where the lender delays the right to exercise foreclosure if the borrower can catch up to the payment schedule in a certain time. The period and payment plan depend on accepted details of the agreement.

[64] "Lessons from the Savings & Loan Debacle: The Case for Further Financial Deregulation," Catherine England, *Regulation: The Cato Review of Business & Government*, Summer 1992.

The U.S. capital market is currently undergoing a restructuring process. The question remains whether policymakers will impede or facilitate that restructuring.

If **Long-Term Capital Management** (LTCM) had a more accurate title, perhaps it would be "First You Build the Monster, and Then the Monster Builds You."

LTCM was a hedge fund founded in 1994 by John Meriwether, the former vice chair and head of bond trading at Salomon Brothers. On its board of directors were Myron Scholes and Robert C. Merton, who shared the 1997 Nobel Memorial Prize in Economic Sciences.

The fund developed highly technical mathematical models to take advantage of fixed-income arbitrage opportunities. The basic idea was that over time the value of long-dated bonds issued a short time apart would tend to become identical. LTCM believed the market was inefficient with respect to the rate at which these bonds approached maturation, speculating that it could profit from the rate differential. In addition, more heavily traded bonds, such as those issued by the U.S. Treasury, would approach the long-term price quicker than less heavily traded, less liquid bonds, creating a pricing inefficiency.

Initially, the company was enormously successful, with annualized returns of over 40% in its first years. However, in 1998 LTCM lost $4.6 billion in less than four months. The fund folded in early 2000.[65]

Lessons learned: Never buy anything smarter than you are. You will have surrendered your decision-making ability. Having a model is different from understanding the drivers of the investment. Elegance of model often has little to do with the return of principal. Modeling is no substitute for management.

Sophisticated financial models are subject to both model and parameter risk. They should be stress-tested and tempered with judgment. Just because there is a brilliant model does not immunize it from dumb mistakes. In point of fact, the model may be so brilliant that others imitated it, thereby changing the competitive environment.

The central public policy issue raised by the LTCM episode is how to constrain excessive leverage more effectively. As events in the summer and fall of 1998 demonstrated, the amount of leverage in the financial system, combined with

---

[65] "Some Lessons on the Rescue of Long-Term Capital Management," Joseph G. Haubrich, *Policy Discussion Paper No. 19*, Federal Reserve Bank of Cleveland, April 2007.

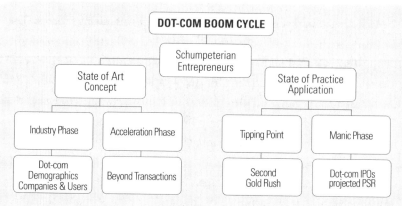

Introductory phase: Demand for the product and its assumptions are mutually reinforced, as existing technologies are reconfigured to meet new opportunities. Sales increased dramatically during the dot-com boom, as commercial applications were applied to a government-sponsored SOP communication bulletin board—the precursor to what we now call the Internet. The business driver was the cheap acquisition of customers. Several factors caused the dot-com bubble. In 1995, the beginning of a major jump in growth of Internet users began, who companies viewed as potential consumers. As a result, numerous Internet start-ups were birthed in the mid- to late-1990s. America was also growing older, with excess discretionary funds to invest in dot-com IPOs.

Acceleration phase: Produces the capability to do something people always wanted to do—if only they had thought of it. Increased profit margins created a mutual dependency between the existing technology and its new application. E-commerce reached 50 million users worldwide in four years. This compares to radio, which took 38 years; personal computers, 16 years; and television, 12 years. The Internet provided solutions that went beyond the transactional benefits of the Electronic Data Interchange[i] and data aggregation benefits of systems like Sabre[ii] to provide low-cost, interactive open markets.

Tipping point: The merger of Silicon Valley and Hollywood. It was California's second "Gold Rush"—this time in search of interactive television. Between April 1992 and July 1993, all major U.S. business magazines had published features on new media and the information superhighway.[iii]

Manic phase: All things were thought to be possible as a result of a new reality. Normative analysis was suspended. Amazon's capitalization was greater than General Eletric's. PSI Net's[iv] value was determined on a projected 12-month price-to-sales ratio. Yet PSI's name lasted longer on the Baltimore football stadium than its symbol lasted on a broker's quote machine.

---

[i] Electronic Data Exchange (EDI) is the computer-to-computer interchange of strictly formatted messages other than monetary instruments (Federal Information Processing Standards Publication). EDI implies a sequence of messages between two parties or computers, transmitted via telecommunications or electronic storage media.
[ii] A computer reservations system/global distribution system.
[iii] "History of the Internet—The Dot-com Bubble," Ian Peter, www.nethistory.info.
[iv] PSINet was among the major players in the commercialization of the Internet until its bankruptcy in 2001 during the dot-com bubble; acquired by Cogent Communications in 2002.

aggressive risk taking, can greatly magnify the negative effects of any event or series of events. By increasing the chance that problems at one financial institution could be transmitted to others, leverage can increase the likelihood of a systemic risk in the financial markets.[66]

The dot-com bubble started when former vice president Al Gore talked about the "information superhighway." In the early 1990s, Hollywood, Silicon Valley, telecommunications carriers, cable companies, and media conglomerates, all became enthusiastic investors—buy high in the hopes of selling higher.

To analyze this phenomenon, I will again illustrate with a modified version of George Soros' boom-bust model (*SFO Magazine*, April 2009).[67] The model contains two segments, a Schumpeterian boom schematic (page 28) and a Minsky bust schematic (page 30). The boom cycle integrates SOP concepts with SOA applications. This changes the terms of competitive engagement and create investment opportunities for early-adapters.

Trend analysis is a function of risk management. Increases in the trend's risk are related to the trend's biases.

The bust segment introduces SOA technology. One of the most important decisions in economics is determining the demand for major capital goods relative to sources of funds from financial institutions and wealthy individuals.

On both sides of the capital investment decision, we have agents who must put a present value on various long-lived assets, which are subject to large potential capital losses.

To evaluate an investment project, the expected cash flows throughout the project's lifetime must be estimated. To rationally compose a portfolio requires estimates of long-term financial asset prices over the planning horizon. The key question confronting the theory of agent choice is, *What do the agents of choice know about the future, and how do they come to know it?*[68]

---

[66] The U.S. President's Working Group on Financial Markets, Hedge Funds, Leverage, and the Lessons of Long-Term Capital Management, April 1999.

[67] Also see "GAAMA: A New Perspective for Emerging Markets," Stephen A. Boyko, *International Journal of Economic Development*, Vol. IV, No. 2, April 2002.

[68] Crotty, James. *Are Keynesian Uncertainty and Macrotheory Compatible? Conventional Decision Making, Institutional Structures, and Conditional Stability in Keynesian Macromodels,* (University of Massachusetts, Amherst, Massachusetts, 1994).

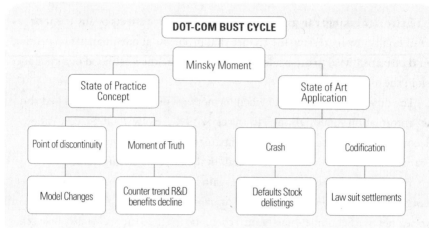

Point of discontinuity: Recognizing the divergence between reality and the new application's presumed benefit. Profits narrow as SOA technological innovations are sought to achieve original forecasts. As illustrated by E*trade's commercials during the 1999 Super Bowl halftime show, advertising expenses grew faster than profits. Super Bowl ads are one of the most expensive types of advertising; choosing this method violates the e-commerce tenet of cheap acquisition of clients. Either E*trade did not know its business, which I do not believe, or the business had changed.

Moment of truth: When research and development reaches the point of diminishing returns, as technology is no longer able to provide greater benefit at less cost. Obsolescence threatens SOP technologies. Weak competitors consolidate through mergers and acquisitions. The dot-com crash of 2000 and 2001 saw great wealth disappear overnight. This was illustrated when online grocer, Streamline, stopped service after thoroughly exhausting financing alternatives. NASDAQ halted trading at $0.16 per share. To make ends meet, Streamline sold its Washington, D.C., and Chicago operations to Peapod, which then was purchased by supermarket giant and foreign direct investor, Royal Ahold.[v]

Codification phase: A retrenchment from overcapacity. Market demand is satisfied at a replacement rate. What was SOA technology becomes a commodity, and the process is repeated. Societal codifications (legal/tax) memorialize the previous trend's biases. Best practices of the preceding trend are codified in the form of new industry rules. Consider high-profile Internet analyst Henry Blodget, who left Merrill Lynch with a severance package estimated at $2 million and a court ruling that limited lawsuits from disgruntled investors who lost money when the Internet-stock bubble burst.[vi]

---

[v] An international group of quality supermarkets and foodservice operators based in the United States and Europe.
[vi] In 2001, Henry Blodget accepted a buyout offer from Merrill Lynch and left the firm.

To fund the development of next generation technology and capital goods, business plans' *pro formas* employed long-term extrapolations based on short-term hyperbolic growth experience. This created unstable, far-from-equilibrium condi-

Google's Post-IPO Performance

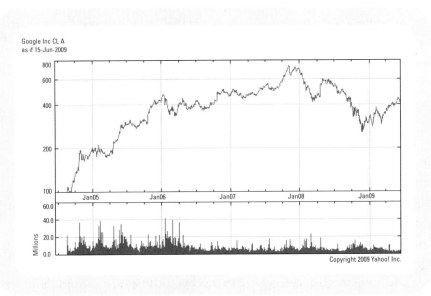

tions, such as the dot-com bust cycle's Minsky Moment. The bust schematic consists of the point of discontinuity, moment of truth, crash, and codification phases.

Bubbles, once broken, are not easily reassembled. The E*trade example on page 30 of the trend's inflection point represents subjective judgment, as the company changed its business model to spend a significant amount to get new customers.

There are other examples to illustrate this shift in sentiment:
- The success tax resulting from the Microsoft's anti-trust suit;
- The Fed tightening in 1996 to curb what Greenspan told the American Enterprise Institute was "irrational exuberance," which caused an increase in interest rates;
- Greater systemic risk from the political uncertainty attendant to the 2000 Presidential election.

In all, there was a point when investors should have become defensive because they recognized the impending Minsky Moment.

Lessons learned: There is no substitute for business experience. Most venture capitalists who gave millions of dollars to bright, ambitious, twenty somethings were simply gambling on the few that would pay off.

Free is an unsustainable business model. The quickest way to go bankrupt is to capture an increasing share of flat-margin business.

Notwithstanding the warning above, could the lessons learned in the past be forgotten when we're wooed by win-win synergies that produce the promise of penny stocks turning into investment fortunes? Will there be another dot-com bubble? A picture of the Google post-IPO stock performance (page 31) suggests a resounding—*yes*!

Enron started as a regional natural gas pipeline company. It was the result of a merger between Houston Natural Gas and InterNorth in 1985. Enron's founder, Kenneth Lay, was credited with transforming the company into the world's largest energy trading company and, at one time, America's fifth-biggest corporation. Enron was quick to exploit opportunities presented by deregulation in the late 1980s, which allowed users to buy gas or electricity from different producers.

Enron became a Wall Street darling. Its value proposition was to capture revenues from merged, deregulated energy externalities and convert those revenues with a premium price-to-earning valuation multiple into a high-flying stock price.

Enron's core business was legitimate and quite beneficial for the marketplace and consumers. Its basic business strategy was known as "asset lite." Enron combined small investments in a capital-intensive industry with derivatives trading and market making.[69]

As its business model developed, Enron became a full-blown over-the-counter (OTC) derivatives trading firm. Illustrative of its asset-lite strategic success was that Enron's OTC derivatives-related business increased more than five-fold during 2000 alone.[70]

---

[69] "Empire of the Sun: An Economic Interpretation of Enron's Energy Business," Christopher L. Culp and Steve H. Hanke, *Policy Analysis*, (Cato Institute, February 23, 2003).

[70] Testimony of Frank Partnoy, professor of law, University of San Diego Law School Senate Hearing, 107–376, Second Session, January 24, 2002, p. 58.

While Enron was successful in its core business—where it had comparative advantage from asymmetrical information—its failure was that it got too clever and did not stick to its knitting. Specifically, Enron used derivatives and special purpose vehicles to manipulate its financial statements in three ways.

First, Enron hid losses it suffered on technology stocks. Second, it hid huge debts incurred from financing unprofitable new businesses. Third, it inflated the value of other troubled businesses, including its new ventures in fiber-optic bandwidth.[71]

As a reaction to Enron's corporate and accounting scandals, The Sarbanes-Oxley Act of 2002 (SOX) was passed. The legislation set new or enhanced standards for all U.S. publicly held[72] company boards, management, and public accounting firms. The act contains 11 titles, or sections, ranging from additional corporate board responsibilities to criminal penalties, and requires the SEC to implement rulings on requirements to comply with the law.

Debate continues over the perceived benefits and costs of SOX. Supporters contend the legislation was necessary and has played a useful role in restoring public confidence in the nation's capital markets.

Opponents claim SOX has reduced America's international competitiveness. These challengers say SOX has introduced an overly complex regulatory environment into U.S. financial markets.[73] It has raised listing costs, inducing many of our innovative companies to seek listing offshore.

Lessons learned: If SOX is as beneficial as supporters claim, why hasn't it ever been cited in SEC enforcement cases? Given the lack of documented violations, it appears SOX's regulatory effect has been to swap errors of commission (SEC enforcement activity) for errors of omission (going offshore).

Further, where were the stock analysts in determining Enron's market value? If journalist Bethany McLean[74] could expose the corrupt business practices of Enron, where were the chartered financial analysts?

---

[71] Ibid.
[72] It does not apply to privately held companies.
[73] *Sustaining New York and the U.S.'s Global Financial Services Leadership*, 2007 McKinsey Report commissioned by New York City Mayor Michael Bloomberg and U.S. Senator Charles Schumer (D, New York).
[74] McLean, now a contributing editor to *Vanity Fair*, worked for *Fortune* when she exposed the Enron scandal. Widely acknowledged as the first journalist to question Enron's inflated stock price, her March 5, 2001, *Fortune* article was titled "Is Enron Overpriced?" She went on to write *Enron: The Smartest Guys in the Room* with Peter Elkind. The book exposes the corrupt business practices of Enron officials.

Finally, how could an energy trading company change its successful asset-lite business model to an asset-intensive model without questions from the board of directors? Someone had to ask why a successful asset-lite strategy was replaced by asset-heavy.

Bernard "Bernie" Madoff (born 1938) is a former non-executive chairman of the NASDAQ stock exchange. In 2009, he pled guilty to an 11-count criminal complaint and was sentenced to 150 years in prison.

In his plea, Madoff admitted to defrauding thousands of investors and was convicted of operating a Ponzi scheme that has been called the largest ever investor fraud committed by a single person. Federal prosecutors estimated client losses, which included fabricated gains, at $64.8 billion.

Madoff founded the Wall Street firm Bernard L. Madoff Investment Securities LLC in 1960 and was its chair until his arrest in December 2008. The firm was one of the top market makers on Wall Street. It bypassed specialist firms by directly executing OTC orders from retail brokers.[75]

According to his company, Madoff was one of the five broker-dealers most closely involved in developing the NASDAQ Stock Market as well as a member of the board of governors of the National Association of Securities Dealers (NASD) and many related committees.

Lessons learned: Madoff's Ponzi scheme is noteworthy for its size and duration. This is a result of the bull market robustness. As Minsky notes, the "Ponzi borrower" borrows based on the belief that the appreciation of the value of the underlying asset will sufficiently refinance the debt. The Ponzi borrower cannot make sufficient payments on interest or principal with the cash flow from investments. Only the appreciating asset value can keep the Ponzi borrower afloat.[76]

But the real genius of Madoff was his knowledge of "culture"—the Jewish culture of the clients he bilked and the SEC culture he conned.

His pitch was consistent with their worldview, so they never asked the tough questions. As long as there was steady, positive appreciation, the "why" and "what" questions satisfactorily preempted the "*how*."

---

[75] "Investors remain amazed over Madoff's sudden downfall," staff writers, *USA Today*, December 15, 2008.
[76] Kindleberger, Charles P., and Robert Aliber. *Manias, Panics and Crashes: A History of Financial Crises*, Fifth Edition, (Wiley Investment Classics, New York, N.Y., 2005) p. 27-28.

There will always be an **affinity scam**—one that targets a particular group based on idiosyncratic traits the perpetrator shares with the group. These traits provide a comparative advantage. In this case, that advantage was knowledge of Jewish culture and heritage. What is troubling from a policy perspective is that the SEC lacked the intellectual diversity that warned red flags were present.

Harry Markopolos, a chartered financial analyst and certified fraud examiner, wrote a warning letter to the SEC on November 7, 2005, and it is a stunning document. In it, Markopolos created a detailed presentation of more than two dozen red flags regarding Madoff's operation. It outlined a specific trail of evidence for the SEC.

Most shocking is the SEC's failure to follow the trail so clearly presented in a 19-page document.[77] In a market characterized by extreme volatility, Madoff hooked his clients and the SEC with a modest but steady return on investment. His clients had achieved success in terms of financial security; they didn't want to lose it. Madoff conveyed to all participants that a return *of* principal was more important than a return *on* principal. He sold "predictability" in a volatile and uncertain market.

The arrival of new SEC Enforcement Director Robert Khuzami in 2009 signaled a strategic move toward specialization of regulation. Khuzami said that based on his experience at the SEC and from recent accounts of the SEC's failings in the Madoff fraud case, he believes, "The move to specialization is a particularly important one. The plain truth is that not every investigator in the Enforcement Division has the background or experience to handle a complex accounting fraud case properly or to recognize a fraud such as that perpetrated by Madoff."[78]

Segmentation of *process*, as compared to segmentation of *products*, is a major step toward the reform of the SEC.

The subprime crash of 2008 was a perfect storm, born from excess good intentions. A modified version of Soros' boom-bust model (*SFO Magazine*, April 2009) is used to illustrate[79] this bubble (page 36).

---

[77] http://www.scribd.com/doc/9189285/Markopolos-Madoff-Complaint.
[78] "Specialization Key to SEC Enforcement Overhaul," Bruce Carton, *Securities Docket*, May 5, 2009.
[79] Also see "GAAMA: A New Perspective for Emerging Markets," Stephen A. Boyko, *International Journal of Economic Development*, Vol. IV, No. 2, April 2002.

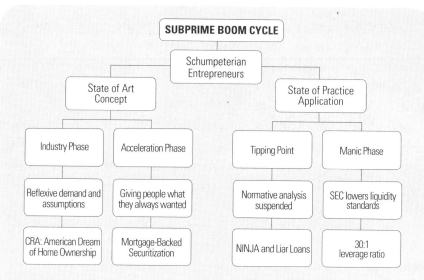

Introductory phase: Demand for home ownership and its assumptions are mutually reinforced. Low- and moderate-income (LMI) borrowers' new home mortgages were financed through the Community Reinvestment Act (CRA). LMI applicants must have very low-, low- or moderate incomes to qualify. Very low-income is defined as below 50% of the area median income (AMI); Low is between 50- 80% of AMI; moderate is below 115% of AMI. Families must be without adequate housing but able to afford housing payments, including principal, interest, taxes, and insurance (PITI).[vii] Applicants must be unable to obtain credit elsewhere, yet have an acceptable credit history. Qualifying repayment ratios are 29% for PITI to 41% for total debt. The CRA employed government and market forces to provide a formulaic solution that enabled federally insured banks and thrifts to increase conventional home loans to LMI borrowers from 14.4% in 1990 to 24.7% in 2001.

Acceleration phase: Gives people the ability to do something they always wanted to do—if only they had thought of it. Increased profit opportunities created a mutual dependency between the existing market for home mortgages and a new application of mortgage-backed securities (MBS). President Bush's domestic vision for his second term was to create an "ownership society." On June 17, 2004, he said, "(I)f you own something, you have a vital stake in the future of our country. The more ownership there is in America, the more vitality there is in America."[viii] Created at Salomon Brothers in the 1980s, the MBS market grew to become a multi-trillion dollar a year business.

Inflection, or **tipping point:** When normative analysis was suspended for loans nicknamed "NINJA" (No Income, No Job, No Assets) and "LIAR," where a lender does not require documentation of employment, income, or credit history. These ill-advised loans must be viewed in the context of the times; Congress cautioned lenders against redlining—the practice of denying financial services based on race, ethnicity, and/or income. Banks accused of redlining faced stiff penalties under the Community Reinvestment Act (CRA[ix]). This law pressured banks to lower long-held industry standards for judging creditworthiness, causing them to make subprime loans to people with poor credit scores.

Manic phase: All things were thought to be possible. A new reality occurred on April 28, 2004, in an SEC meeting. At that time, the capital leverage ratio was allowed to increase from 12:1 to in excess of 30:1. The net capital and leverage ratio requirements determine the speed at which the market can operate. Raising the leverage ratio meant that an 8.5% capital cushion was reduced to 3.3%. Given the speed with which 3x derivatives work, the reduced capitalization cushion provided scant protection against bear raids in financial securities. The net capital and leverage ratio requirements are to upward pressure of the boom cycle as circuit breakers are to the downward pressure of the bust cycle; both slow throughput to ensure an orderly and rational market. Reducing liquidity standards put the capital market on steroids and allowed the bubble to reach manic proportions.

[vii] *Catalog of Federal Domestic Assistance.*
[viii] *Presidential news release, June 17, 2004.*
[ix] *Housing and Community Development Act of 1977.*

The model contains two segments, a Schumpeterian entrepreneurial boom schematic and a Minsky Moment bust schematic. The boom cycle integrates SOP concepts with SOA applications. This changes the terms of competitive engagement and creates investment opportunities for early adapters. Trend analysis is a function of risk management. Increases in the trend's risk are related to the trend's biases.

The bust schematic finds SOA concepts introduced to change the terms of competitive engagement.

Having picked the low-hanging fruit, practitioners increase market activity by extrapolating the SOA concepts' hyperbolic growth projections. To get funding to develop next generation technology and capital goods, business plans' financial *pro formas* employed long-term extrapolations based on short-term hyperbolic growth experience.

This resulted in unstable, far-from-equilibrium conditions. Eventually the Minsky Moment occurs with the bursting of the bubble. As **Subprime Bust Cycle** on page 38 illustrates, the bust schematic consists of the point of discontinuity, moment of truth, crash, and codification phases.

Lessons learned: Policymakers' two-dimensional remedies were slow to respond because they lacked the three-dimensional conceptual ability to tackle problems comprehensively.

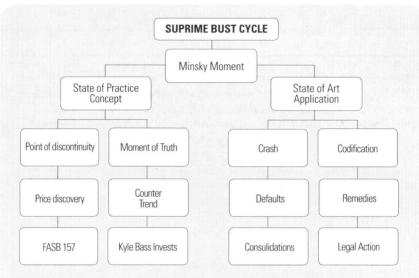

Point of discontinuity: When the divergence between reality and the bubble's presumed benefit was recognized. Some of the tranches[x] of mortgage-backed securities were worthless. Advanced price-discovery metrics were created from Financial Accounting Standards Board 157,[xi] which defined fair value and established higher standards for AAA ratings. On April 2, 2009, FASB "mark-to-market" accounting rules were revised, allowing companies more latitude in determining the fair value of their assets.

Moment of truth: When J. Kyle Bass, a Dallas hedge fund manager, committed capital to his theory about a looming housing market meltdown. Bass bet on a crash in residential real estate by trading securities based on subprime mortgages to the least credit-worthy borrowers. Bass soon earned billions, as delinquencies on home loans made to people with poor credit reached record levels and prices for mortgage-backed securities plunged.

Crash phase: Homeowners were no longer able to support the indebtedness of their mortgage and/or home equity line. The net result of ill-advised NINJA and LIAR loans was to give renters property rights: *If I put no money down and make a mortgage payment, what is the difference, other than the fact that I got a free warrant for the real estate gain by categorizing it as a mortgage payment?*

Weak financial institutions consolidated through mergers and acquisitions. Some of these arrangements, like Bank of America Corp. and Merrill Lynch & Co., could be described as shotgun weddings. Bank of America Chief Executive Officer Kenneth Lewis testified that the federal government threatened to remove board members at his bank if it reneged on a promise to acquire Merrill Lynch, despite the crumbling financial state of the latter. Lawmakers accused federal regulators of a gross misuse of power in orchestrating merger—with U.S. taxpayers footing the $20 billion bill. A panel has investigated whether federal officials pressured Lewis and urged him to keep quiet about Merrill Lynch's financial problems. Lewis contends that divulging such information would have violated his fiduciary duty to the bank's shareholders. In testimony before the panel, Lewis said publicly for the first time that his job was threatened after he expressed second thoughts about the merger. Lewis said federal regulators and Hank Paulson, then U.S. Treasury secretary, made clear that if the bank reneged on its promise, they would force his ouster and that of board members.[xii]

Codification phase: Addresses the most grievous boom-bust errors. Reinstating the **uptick rule** has been proposed. This rule prohibits short selling securities, except on an uptick. Rule 10a-1 of the Securities Exchange Act provides that, subject to certain exceptions, a listed security may be sold short (A) at a price above the last selling price (plus tick), or (B) at the last sale price if it is higher than the last different price (zero-plus tick). Short sales are not permitted on minus ticks or zero-minus ticks. The logic is that short selling without a plus-tick rule takes liquidity out of the market by diminishing bid-side depth. The rule went into effect in 1938 and was removed when Rule 201 Regulation SHO became effective in 2007. In 2009, the reintroduction of the uptick rule was widely debated, and proposals for a form of its reintroduction by the SEC went to public comment.[xiii]

---

[x] A piece or portion of structured financing.

[xi] FASB 157 defines fair value, establishes a framework for measuring fair value in generally accepted accounting principles, and expands disclosures about fair-value measurements. Until recently, there were different definitions of fair value and limited guidance for applying those definitions in Generally Accepted Accounting Principles, notes FASB. Guidance also was dispersed among accounting pronouncements that require fair-value measurements.

[xii] "Bank of America CEO: Feds Pressured Bank to Buy Merrill Lynch," Fox News, June 11, 2009.

[xiii] "U.S. SEC to Consider About 4 Short-Sale Proposals," Rachelle Younglai, *Reuters*, April 6, 2009; "SEC Votes to Seek Comments on All Proposed Short-Sale Rules," *Wall Street Journal*, April 8, 2009.

It is the difference between using maps and global positioning systems. Having GPS conceptual capability to govern on-the-fly is a prerequisite for regulating global, robust markets. To illustrate, ProShares UltraShort Financials (symbol: SKF) are exchange-traded funds (ETFs) that correspond to twice the inverse of the daily performance of the Dow Jones U.S. Financials. Yet what multidimensional governance alternatives were innovated to monitor SKF's negative 200% impact?

PART I TAKEAWAYS

Renewed calls for GSA-type governance—as argued and hoped for from a diverse group of policy commentators—are understandable given the level of uncertainty and anxiety associated with the 2008 subprime and housing crises. However, is GSA given undeserved credit? We will never know what might have happened if GSA had not been repealed; the world changed, and different pathways were estab-

Markets vs. Firms

STRUCTURE / CHARACTERISTICS	MARKET	FIRM
Structure	Horizontal	Vertical
Production	Transactions	Goods and Services
Transparency	Disclosure	Trade secrets
Operational costs	Infrastructure	Inventory
Transaction costs	Disintermediated	Imbedded
Reform	Regulation and/or Infrastructure	Redesign products and/or Retrain people

As shown above, markets and firms are different. You reform **firms** by retraining or removing management and/or redesigning products (i.e. General Motors). You reform **markets** via regulatory and/or infrastructure enhancements. Instead of changing management and providing a report for recommended action, as was the case with LTCM, policymakers took a presumptive leap, believing their recommendations should be codified as best practices. SOX provides a caution against imbedding costs through rule writing. After Enron, regulators piled on compliance earmarks to address their needs rather than the market's needs. Where were the SOX violations in the subprime crisis? The promised benefits seem to have gone, but the higher costs linger.

lished to accommodate those changes. Therefore, we cannot assume GSA could have dealt with market occurrences without difficulty. Further, investor pathways have shifted to a Metcalfe network. There are global investors with new, innovative products, and their presence has forever altered the nature of the financial services industry.

As illustrated **Financial Crashes and Crises** on page 21, SOX was primarily a reaction to a number of major corporate and accounting scandals, including those of Enron, Tyco International, Adelphia, and WorldCom.

SOX's regulatory efficacy is problematic. It mischaracterizes the initial condition by prescribing remedies for *firm* maladies to be instituted as *market* best practices. This rule writing creates shareholder rights (commands) disproportionate to shareholder responsibilities (incentives), resulting in a moral hazard that subsidizes free riding and rent seeking.

The one-size-fits-all, deterministic governance regime holds that investors are risk averse. That is, investors want to avoid risk unless adequately compensated for it. So if two investments have the same expected return, the one with the lower perceived risk will be preferred. A riskier investment has to have a higher expected return to provide an incentive for a risk-averse investor to select it.

While this is a valid, normative portion of the universe, it is not necessarily so for the "tails" of the population distribution. If, like the NINJA mortgagees, you have nothing—no skin in the game—you have nothing to lose. Your home investment was a lottery ticket.

Likewise for the other extreme distribution, if you can sell AAA-predictability in a volatile and uncertain market, the upside is so great that adverse occurrences are merely a cost of doing business. Wall Street executives were so highly compensated, they could engage in financial brinksmanship; when you make billions, million dollar losses are paid from petty cash. During the subprime bubble, the tails of the bell-curve wagged the normative investor universe.

Markets are coordinated pricing systems that allocate voluntary exchanges between consumers, workers, and owners of production. They are nonlinear, dynamic systems that involve:

1. The exchange of goods and services, with associated property and contracts;
2. Communication of the prospective transaction's terms and conditions;
3. Information on the level of demand that exists for the product; and
4. Infrastructure and procedures to settle and clear transactions.[80]

Markets are open in function (i.e., disclosure and transparency) and horizontal in structure when they reach maturity.

Conversely, **firms** are non-market solutions. These economic actors transform inputs into outputs for use by other economic agents. They internalize transaction costs and/or *infomediation* products (those that make it easier to get information) and related transactional processes.

Firms shift the cost burden in favor of their comparative advantage. They are organized to perform integrated functions that otherwise might be outsourced to a competitive marketplace. Firms tend to be closed in function (i.e., trade secrets and barriers to entry) and vertical in structure when they reach maturity.

---

[80] Peters, Edgar. *Chaos and Order in the Capital Markets: A New View of Cycles, Prices, and Market Volatility*, (Wiley, New York, N.Y. 1996)

Asymmetrical information deals with the study of decisions in transactions, where one party has more or better information than another.

But it is one thing to have access to such information; it is another thing to be capable of processing it. Markopoulos provided the SEC with an excellent road map for investigating Madoff. However, due to a lack of the unique and highly specialized forensic auditing skills necessary for fraud detection, little resulted from Markopoulos' Herculean effort.

What makes America great is that every adult has the unencumbered right to purchase his or her own nightmare. If it seems too good to be true, chances are it is; a bill for payment will always be presented.

Be alert for the "Minsky Moment." Like a great athlete, visualize the causes and your exit scenario. If you are in a loss position when the moment occurs, that first loss in a bursting bubble is usually your cheapest.

PART TWO

Best Practice Governance

BEST PRACTICE GOVERNANCE

Calls for systemic change the U.S. capital markets should begin with the recognition and attendant disclosure of the prevailing economic environment as either determinate, or probable, or indeterminate, or improbable. Thereafter, logic suggests segmenting governance regimes for market realities; it is ridiculous to shoe horn diverse economic environments into one-size-fits-all, monopolistic governance.

Part II explores governance problem solving by establishing analytical structures and metrics. Regulation is primarily a function of pricing and practices, where a complainant can allege he or she was overcharged and/or misled. Governance selects appropriate commands for the incentive set available in the economy. This balances incentives derived from shareholder responsibilities with the command costs attendant to shareholder rights.

Any proposed changes to capital market governance must be real—not merely bureaucratic wordsmithing that changes a comma into a semicolon. Reformers often pour gasoline on the fire by raising regulatory standards ill suited to the problem(s) at hand; remember SOX, the reform to end all reforms.

The problem is the monopolistic nature of the one-size-fits-all regulatory model, which thwarts the natural tendency of markets to segment. Vertical, command-and-control regulatory metrics immobilize capital by limiting horizontal market alternative solutions.

A political system that requires immediate solutions in reaction to publicized crises exacerbate such biases, as illustrated by the S&L meltdown and the resultant TARP. It has cost U.S. taxpayers nearly $1 trillion to learn we need regulatory change. If that amount was required to save top-tier companies, what funding remains for the entrepreneurial enterprises that will create tomorrow's alternative energy, stem-cell research, educational innovation, and more?

As markets become more robust, consumers seek financial instruments tailored with increasing precision to meet their needs. Markets tend to segment into different groups of stakeholders. These stakeholders respond to material information with a high degree of correlation, which is measurable and accessible through different regulatory protocols. Necessary for operational effectiveness is transparent disclosure as to the distinction between the determinate and indeterminate economic environments.

Economist Frank H. Knight made famous this distinction in his seminal book, *Risk, Uncertainty, and Profit* (1921). In brief, he asserts that risk is present when future events occur with measurable probability, while uncertainty is present when the likelihood of future events is indefinite or incalculable.

To ensure best-practice governance, policymakers should balance stakeholder rights with stakeholder responsibilities by disclosing the underlying economic environment and its related segmented governance regime.

DO GOVERNANCE PROBLEM(S) EXIST? IF SO, WHAT ARE THEY?

Let's start the analysis by defining and describing the terms "governance" and "problem."

Governance is the set of processes, customs, policies, laws, and institutions affecting the way an enterprise is directed, administered, and controlled. It also includes the relationships among the many stakeholders and the goals by which stakeholders assert their rights through an elected board of directors and management. It is a system of checks and balances designed to ensure that managers are just as vigilant on behalf of long-term stakeholder value as they would be if their own money were at risk.[1]

During the course of an U.S. Agency for International Development consulting assignment in Yalta to develop the Ukrainian capital market, I was part of a conference panel discussion on corporate governance. I was scheduled give the summation of a speaker's remarks and moderate the question and answer session from 3 to 3:45 p.m. By 3:15, I was still in the on-deck circle, amusing myself by watching the audience being overtaken with "church-pew nods." There is only so much governance a person can withstand until entropy occurs.

This happened all the time at these conferences, and I normally would have sipped my mineral water and waited. But this time there was a sense of urgency, as a scheduled tour of Yalta and the Livadia Palace was to begin at 4 p.m. The palace was the summer home of the last of the Russian tsars, Nikolai II. In 1945, it hosted the Yalta Conference, where British Prime Minister Winston Churchill, U.S. President Franklin Roosevelt, and Joseph Stalin, general secretary of the U.S.S.R.'s Communist Party, met to chart post-war Europe.

---

[1] Dignam, Alan and Lowry, John. *Company Law*, Fifth Edition, (Oxford University Press USA, New York, N.Y., 2008) p. 350-365.

At 3:30 p.m., I ascended the podium a determined man. It was obvious that "Agenda A" was scrapped. I thanked the presenter for giving a very learned and *thorough* commentary on corporate governance. I then informed the audience I would provide an abbreviated summary review, sort of a *CliffsNotes* presentation.

This automatically captured their curiosity. Ukrainians, like most foreigners, love the American culture, irrespective of their feelings toward the U.S. government. Therefore, after a brief description of *CliffsNotes*—my preferred study method for college—I launched into my encapsulation of "corporate governance."

I started with my belief that governance can best be achieved with incentives, such as in a 25-to-one P/E ratio. *Does everyone understand what a P/E ratio is?* I asked. No response. I explained that a P/E ratio, or price-to-earnings ratio of a stock, is a measure used to determine common equity valuation. You calculate the P/E ratio by dividing a company's market capitalization by its net income.

A higher P/E ratio means that investors are willing to pay more for each unit of net income, creating greater value when compared to one with lower P/E ratio. This brought a mixture of nods and sotto voce agreements from the audience. Why? Because at 25-to-1, the CEO can't steal that much. It is in the CEO's self-interest to build the stock account and pay taxes rather than build an offshore bank account. *Skinchilla sprava*[2] as they say in downtown Kiev. Does anyone have any questions?

Oh, and the Livadia Palace was well worth the price of admission.

For our purposes we will view governance is defined as a commercial problem-solving process designed to maximize stakeholder value. It should be noted that the text will focus on the incentives for good governance as much as the rules for good governance.

Now let's analyze the term "problem." **Problem solving** is the linchpin connecting commerce and compliance. While teaching a financial management course several years ago, I was surprised by the number of vague and/or ambiguous[3] conclusions reached in case analyses by Master of Business Administration degree students. These deficiencies were not the result of a lack of effort or

---

[2] "The deal is done."
[3] Peters, Edgar. *Complexity, Risk, and Financial Markets*, (John Wiley & Sons, New York, NY., 2001) p. 29-35. Vagueness is the result of imprecise data that supports all alternatives. Ambiguity is the inability to choose among alternatives due to insufficient, confusing, and/or conflicting data.

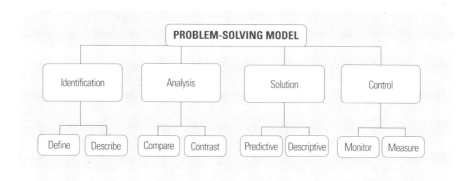

unfamiliarity with the course content. Quite to the contrary, industrious students often suffered from information overload as they tried to substitute quantity of subject matter for a lack of analytical rigor.

By ignoring a 1,500-word limit on the case study executive summary, approximately half of the students learned that violating a budgeting constraint carries consequences. While the word constraint focused the thought process, case presentations still lacked the analytical precision needed to concretize a mission statement.

To address this limitation, I announced to the students during one class session that we would begin work on a "business dictionary" project. Our specific task was to define the word **problem**. It is interesting to note that in five years teaching MBA students, I had only a handful who could envision an abstract model for defining the word "problem."

We all have problems. Problem solving has two prerequisites: the recognition of an adverse condition; and procedures with which to rectify the adverse condition. Our problem-solving success depends on how creative we are in developing an effective (ability to solve) and efficient (minimal expenditure of time, cost, and effort) process.

The **Problem-Solving Model** (above) consists of four conceptual constructs, each having two distinct binary benchmarks. Specifically, the model consists of:
- A way to identify a problem, with the benchmarks of define and describe;
- A method to analyze the problem, with the benchmarks of compare and contrast;
- A plan to solve the problem, with the benchmarks of predictive and descriptive (profiling);
- And a method to **control** the problem, with the benchmarks of monitor and measure.

You will note the similarities between dual or binary benchmarks and the test questions many of us remember from elementary school. When your third-grade

Generic Demonstration Matrix

DEPENDENT CONCEPTUAL CONSTRUCT \ INDEPENDENT CONCEPTUAL CONSTRUCT	BINARY BENCHMARK PRIMARY CHOICE COLUMN B	BINARY BENCHMARK SECONDARY CHOICE COLUMN C
Binary benchmark Primary Choice Row 2	Dynamic Byproduct Solution B2	Dynamic Byproduct Solution C2
Binary benchmark Secondary Choice Row 3	Dynamic Byproduct Solution B3	Dynamic Byproduct Solution C3

teacher asked you "define and describe" something or to "compare and contrast" to objects or ideas, she was asking you to solve a problem in stages. Improving your ability to solve problems and make decisions is widely recognized as invaluable.

A problem is a measured observance outside a normative operating zone. That is, a problem causes you to deviate from your course or plan.

To illustrate, consider a state trooper monitoring traffic on an interstate highway. The Department of Motor Vehicles (DMV) describes a normative operating zone in terms of commands that are appropriate for a given level of traffic and operating conditions. **Commands** are a combination of standards and rules that reflexively control behavior. Rules and standards can be perceived as alternative mechanisms through which governance objectives are satisfied.

As a result, the DMV outlines a normative operating zone through a variety of commands, such as set speed minimums and maximums. The state trooper screens oncoming traffic with a radar gun to determine whether motorists are complying with the speed limit (plus or minus a 5-mile per hour tolerance margin) and prudent driving protocols. Drivers in excess of the speed limit, driving recklessly, and/or driving too slowly in the left lane pose problems that must be addressed. In other words, failure to adhere to traffic laws is the measured observance outside a normative operating zone—the problem. The DMV establishes a governance system as a way to maintain order. The state trooper enforces this system, with some room for flexibility.

Problem analysis involves comparing and contrasting the results from a selection of "MILD" techniques—an acronym that stands for:

- **Modeling** (mathematics, matrices, and physical representations)
- **Investigative** (brainstorming and reverse engineering)

- **Logic** (decision tree and "If I do X, then Y will happen" reasoning)
- **Data mining**

This text utlizes data mining and matrix analysis. Both are reflexive functions similar to multiplication and division. **Matrix analysis** often illustrates a solution path, while **data mining** is used to support the proof. Economic proofs are rarely proven true. No matter how many market tests seem to agree with a theory, it may still be wrong. On the other hand, a single contrary experiment can be used to invalidate an entrepreneurial business model.[4]

Data mining[5] uses information extraction techniques to accumulate and separate facts from assumptions. Facts are empirical, practical truths, whereas assumptions are beliefs without observed evidence. In data mining, facts are correlated to format recognizable information patterns. Hypotheses are suppositions—limited statements regarding cause and effect that refer to the knowledge you have before conducting an experiment.

Predictions are initial conditions (inputs) combined with a hypothesis; based on what you know and what you can foresee, you can make guesses about the outcome of the experiment. Explanations are end conditions (outputs) combined with hypotheses. The data-mining methodology collects facts that are mutually exclusive and collectively exhaustive.[6] Facts are then formatted to transform data into information. Thereafter, tests (input/output analyses) are conducted to validate the hypotheses for solving a particular problem.

Models present a simplified version of a complex reality. For example, you provide AOL's mapquest.com with the starting and ending points of a trip. It then formats this data to select the most efficient solution and provides you with a map and written instructions. So your hypothesis—I can get driving directions for my trip from Map Quest—is accompanied by the prediction that the site will provide accurate, easy to understand instructions.

---

[4] George Soros refers to this as "radical fallibility" (*Open Society*, 2000); "Introduction to the Scientific Method," Appendix E, Dr. Frank Wolfs, 2002, University of Rochester Department of Physics; "Epistemology and Economic Methodology," lecture by H. Stephen Gardner, Herman Brown Professor of Economics, Baylor University, 2009.

[5] From Two Crows Consulting data-mining firm, Potomac, Maryland. Typical data-mining applications include market segmentation, customer profiling, fraud detection, evaluation of retail promotions, and credit risk analysis.

[6] Raisel, Ethan M. *The McKinsey Way: Using the Techniques of the World's Top Strategic Consultants to Help You and Your Business*, (McGraw-Hill, New York, N.Y., 1998) p. 187.

Problematic Governance Matrix

QUANTITATIVE ANALYTICS / QUALITATIVE CONTROLS	OVER-REGULATION TOO MANY RULES (BEST-PRACTICES) TOO HIGH STANDARDS	UNDER-REGULATION TOO FEW RULES (BEST-PRACTICES) TOO LOW STANDARDS
Ineffective: not knowing the correct strategy	Rule writing that produced SOX	One-size-fits-all regulation
Inefficient: not executing tactics correctly	SOX drives SME IPOs offshore to London AIM and Australian ASSOB	2-D governance for 3-D market realties

Perhaps your hypothesis is based on the site's reputation, while your prediction is based on past experiences using the service. Using the directions is the test, which provides you with your explanation.

Models are used to structure and test validity of the hypothesis. The **Generic Demonstration Matrix** on page 48 models the functionality of matrix analysis.

The use of the terms "independent conceptual construct" and "dependent conceptual construct" are similar but subtly different. They are used to distinguish between two types of variables being considered. The matrix separates them into those available at the start of a process and those being created by it, where the value of the dependent construct is a function of the independent construct.

The title, **Generic Demonstration Matrix,** describes the issue to be analyzed. Both independent and dependent conceptual constructs have binary benchmarks that interact with each other to form a dynamic byproduct solution.

For example, Binary Benchmark Primary Choice Column B interacts with the second row of Binary Benchmark Primary Choice, creating solution "B2." The array of solutions—B2, C2, B3, and C3—are then arranged in sequence and timing to be implemented and provide an optimal descriptive solution set.

For a practical example, consider the **Problematic Governance Matrix** (above). This three-by-three matrix consists of qualitative analytics for problem solving, with the related binary benchmarks of over-regulation and under-regulation, and quantitative analytics, with the related benchmarks of ineffectiveness and inefficiency.

Combining the binary benchmarks of ineffective governance and over-regulation results in the matrix byproduct of rule writing. Such was the case with SOX, which has proved to be the height of rule writing.

Governance vs. Rule Writing

GOVERNANCE: ORGANIZING PROCESS FOR CAPITAL MARKET DECISION MAKING	RULE WRITING: PROSCRIPTIVE DESCRIPTION OF AN ADVERSE MARKET CONDITION
Comprehensive problem solving	Proscriptive description
Randomness	Deterministic
Segmented: Cash flow and Correlation	One-size-fits-all
3-D systemic knowledge	2-D commercial censorship
Market-driven net benefit	Rent-seeking protection cost

In this sense, **rule writing** produces a narrow-minded description of an undesirable situation. It does not necessarily produce a net benefit and should not be considered synonymous with governance. Instead, rule writing is unprepared policymaking that merely places a temporary bandage on the problem. It expects buy-in from society by describing the undesirable situation and prefacing it by saying "don't do this."

Former Securities Exchange Commission Secretary Jonathan G. Katz commented that when "the SEC adopts a rule, it believes it has solved whatever problem it is addressing. ... The solution is to rethink the rulemaking process. Instead of assuming, as lawyers do, that rules are self-effectuating, the SEC should adopt a scientific approach."[7]

For example, while SOX has increased compliance costs, it appears to have provided little benefit in the subprime crash and the Madoff Ponzi scheme. **Governance vs. Rule Writing** (above) compares and contrasts the two.

Matrix problem analysis compares and contrasts byproduct solutions that are similar in nature and essential to understanding the problem of sub-optimal governance. The matrix connection of too low standards for information correlation and ineffective strategy results in the problem of one-size-fits-all regulation, which combines risk and uncertainty. This results in asymmetrical information and non-correlation.

Inefficient over-regulation subsidizes offshore competitors to create errors of omission. Finally inefficient, under-regulation from two-dimensional metrics

---

[7] "Rules Are Not Sacred, Principles Are," Jonathan G. Katz, *Wall Street Journal*, August 8, 2006.

that have to address three-dimensional market realities lack processing speed. (This is similar to using a folded map instead of a global positioning device to navigate downtown traffic during rush hour.) These constructs are then subdivided into binary benchmarks to identify the boundaries of the domain(s) to be examined.

In governance we find an organizing process for capital market decision making. It is comprehensive in nature because it addresses the root cause of the problem. Viewed from the scope of randomness, governance encompasses both determinate and indeterminate underlying economic environments.

Comprehensive governance is based on codified best practices in support of the **FLITE model's** principles of fairness, liquidity, integration, transparency, and efficiency. It provides a societal net benefit in terms of greater wealth to an expanding investor base. By emphasizing education to qualify investors, comprehensive governance reflexively reduces the number of noise traders by ensuring shareholder rights (commands) are proportionate to shareholder responsibilities (incentives). Otherwise, the system allows for the creation of subsidies that foster inefficient free riding and rent seeking.

Indeterminate issuers and related financial products are associated with negative cash flow. These enterprises focus on managing their burn rate—the speed with which they will use up shareholder capital. This compares to positive cash flow companies, which seek to maximize value. If the underlying economic environment differs (positive/negative cash flow), the issuer universe should be segmented to better correlate information. The higher the degree of information correlation, the more efficient the communication is in providing systemic commands.

Innovation is the hallmark of capital markets, yet innovative solutions for global markets create greater complexity. Complexity begets uncertainty, as innovative financial products evolve from earlier, simpler versions to address heretofore uncertain and unforeseeable circumstances.

One-size-fits-all, deterministic governance regimes are disproportionate to uncertain issuers. Thus, it is not surprising that many issuers have gravitated to offshore markets like the London Stock Exchange's Alternative Investment Market (AIM).

Established in 1995, this market provides a good illustration of an offshore market externality. Since inception, more than 2,200 companies have been admitted, and more than £24 billion has been raised collectively. In 2005, the London

Stock Exchange attracted from the United States to AIM a record 19 companies, which raised a combined total of $2.126 million.[8] At the peak of the market in 2007, there were 76 U.S. companies from many sectors—everything from finance and insurance to media and automobile parts. But the most popular areas are renewable energy, software, and biotechnology companies.[9]

Mike Fletcher of European investment bank Altium said one of the reasons so many companies move to AIM is because it allows them to avoid the reams of paperwork and heavy costs associated with a U.S. flotation.

"Companies are finding American markets increasingly difficult since SOX introduced major changes to the corporate governance and financial practice regime in the U.S., resulting in inflated costs," he said. "We are seeing an increasing number of U.S. companies exploring the possibility of a U.K. listing as a result. But it's not just Americans that are being turned off by SOX. U.K. utility giant United Utilities has just announced that it is to de-list from the New York Stock Exchange in an attempt to reduce costs and relieve its regulatory burden."

So as America seeks to stimulate the development of "green" cars and other innovative technologies, SOX-type regulatory hurdles create incentives to go offshore.

Much of the offshore migration is attributed to SOX. A market-driven conceptual change must take place if the U.S. capital markets are to remain competitive in a global economy.

INFORMATION + INNOVATION = SMART REFORM

It has been said that the emphasis of smart reform is to add more information, not more regulatory costs. Issuers are voting with their feet. Lists of rules, such as SOX, that do not represent codified best practices degenerate to commercial censorship.

In such an environment, rent-seeking[10] protection costs are greater than the benefits provided. It is the baseball admonition: Unless the minor league feeder

---

[8] London Stock Exchange.
[9] "United Kingdom: Taking Aim To The US," *Mondaq*, October 21, 2007.
[10] Rent seeking occurs when a company, organization, or individual uses resources to obtain an economic gain from others without returning benefits to society through wealth creation. An example is when a company lobbies for government loans subsidies, grants, or tariff protections. These activities don't create any societal benefit; they just redistribute taxpayers resources to a special-interest group.

system is maintained, all that will remain is Old Timers Day[11] (e.g., General Electric, Proctor & Gamble). Innovative companies go offshore to reduce compliance costs. If this trend continues, the United States may eventually become an extract economy, with most of the value-added components being done elsewhere.

Problem solutions are either predictive or descriptive. Good governance combines vision with pragmatism by not making the "perfect" the enemy of the "good." It takes a Darwinian path of least resistance for the sequencing and timing to prototype, test, measure pricing volatility, and produce models of commands, all of which is proportionate to a given level of incentives available in the economy.

A predictive solution is an equation or set of rules that makes it possible to forecast an unseen or unmeasured discrete value (the dependent variable or output) from other known values (independent variables or inputs).

For example, given the independent variables of the radius of a circle and the statistical estimation used to approximate the value for the constant, p (pi=3.14), we can determine a unique value for the dependent variable of the circle's area from the equation: area of circle = pr^2.

Using the mathematical technique of integration, we can perturb or manipulate the formula from a two- to a three-dimensional format to determine the volume of a sphere from the equation: volume = $4/3\ pr^3$. Each equation provides a specific answer.

A **descriptive solution** is a proposal for the range of prospective solutions. William B. Arthur's[12] work on path dependencies provides a good descriptive illustration. Arthur states that the market makes mistakes, and there are essentially three pathways by which we correct these mistakes.

One, there are mistakes that correct themselves—like eating bad food, which the body usually purges in self-defense. Two, there are mistakes that we live with, like the QWERTY typewriter keyboard (there are better keyboard models, but

---

[11] Refers to the Major League Baseball tradition of devoting the time preceding a team's weekend game to celebrate retired players.

[12] Arthur, William B., *Increasing Returns and Path Dependence in the Economy*, (University of Michigan Press, Ann Arbor) from introduction by Kenneth J. Arrow. Arthur (born 1945), an Irish economist, influenced and described the modern theory of increasing returns. He is a sought-after speaker on economics and Complexity Theory.

the benefit isn't worth the effort to change). And three, there are those mistakes that require a remedy. By mixing risk-uncertainty distinctions within a one-size-fits-all regime,[13] we continue to pay for rule-writing expenses even though the perceived problem may have self-corrected or was later determined to be manageable without requiring further remediation.[14]

To illustrate the difference between predictive and descriptive models, consider the Wright brother's dilemma. They could have defined the "problem" in a *predictive* manner: create a specific solution for building a heavier-than-air machine that flies reliably (Six Sigma[15]) under its own power.

However, the Wright brothers chose to frame the definition of their problem *descriptively*—in terms of a societal need for an airline industry, not engineering capabilities. Instead of obtaining a patent for a specific airplane to monopolize the embryonic air industry, the brothers pragmatically patented a process that included but was not limited to:

- How much force is needed to lift the plane?
- What optimal wing configuration is needed for a given level of speed to generate the necessary lift?
- How do you go up and down (pitch)?
- How do you turn (yaw)?
- How do you keep the plane from tipping (roll)?[16]

The Wright brothers recognized that anyone who built an airplane would need to control the elements of flight. Their process patent allowed them to collect royalties from anyone who built airplanes. They encouraged others to build planes, while they built an industry. To this end, the Wright brothers published,

---

[13] FASB illustrated the move away from the one-size-fits-all mindset in amending FASB 157. FASB 157 segments the valuation inputs by whether they are observable, reflecting market activity from data that is marked-to-the model (based on actual transactions from an active market); observable, reflecting comparable market activity; or unobservable, reflecting reporting entity assumptions.

[14] "Path Dependence, Lock-In, and History," S. J. Liebowitz, University of Texas at Dallas, and Stephen E. Margolis, North Carolina State University.

[15] General Electric's zero-defect standard for manufacturing excellence.

[16] U.S. Patent No. 821,393, "O. & W. Wright Flying Machine," application filed March 23, 1903.

gave demonstrations, and sold airplane assembly plans. Their razor-blade strategy was to encourage others to build the *products* of the industry while they perfected the *processes*.[17]

The control function combines common sense with common practice to develop best practices that are relevant to the cultural experience and proportionate to the current level of commercial activity. The monitoring benchmark ascertains the solution's inputs to ensure that participants are prepared and "know what to do." This construct tests for preparedness by eliminating ambiguity resulting from insufficient data, unclear choices, and/or conflicting results that cannot differentiate among choices. The measuring benchmark also determines the solution's outputs by ensuring that actors "do what they know."

PART II TAKEAWAYS

It may be too early to reach definitive conclusions about the subprime crash of 2008. It took 10 years for the U.S. General Accounting Office and San Francisco Federal Reserve Bank to provide a loss total for the 1987 market crash. Even then, there still was a 20% differential ($1 trillion vs. $800 billion). What may be more meaningful is whether an inflection point[18] has been reached, where the capital market provides diminishing net benefits in the face of larger and more frequent market dislocations.

If this is so, what needs to take place to do the right things for governance effectiveness? A required first step would be to segment the current one-size-fits-all governance regime to better process the randomness of the underlying economic environments. Segmenting governance into separate areas that apply to predictable, probabilistic, and uncertain regimes provides enhanced information correlation from which to issue best-practice commands. This would reduce attempts to govern through rule writing and help decrease compliance expenses that become imbedded as a fixed cost of doing business.

Market-driven metrics are needed to develop a three-dimensional governance structure. There are growing inefficiencies from having regulators govern with two-dimensional metrics in a three-dimensional world.

---

[17] "Cutting to the Chase," Stephen A. Boyko, *Pace University Business Journal*, May 5, 2005.
[18] An inflection point, or inflexion, is a point on a curve at which the curvature changes sign. Imagine driving a vehicle along a winding road; inflexion is the point at which the steering wheel is momentarily "straight" when being turned.

The U.S. capital market regulatory structure has become a hierarchical, command-and-control process similar to the former Soviet Union's *Gosplan*; it lacked the information system to restructure. It was unable to address effectively the complexities required by the Information Age.

U.S. regulators find themselves in a similar situation. Their linear budgetary resources cannot satisfy the exponential demands required by global capital markets with complex, innovative products.

What is ironic is that having demonstrated the virtues of capitalism, American policymakers are now trying to recreate the governance regime of European ancestry. Napoleonic Code governs Europe, where an activity is prohibited unless expressly permitted. English Common Law is the reverse: Unless an activity is expressly prohibited, it is permitted. America took this "openness" and added the concept of "sweat equity" as an incentive to the settlers of the frontier.

By combining risk and uncertainty, policymakers render SOX-type rule writing disproportionate for smaller issuers and revert to Napoleonic Code. Are our policymakers fostering what our ancestors rejected?[19]

When dealing in the realm of politics, historical context and logic are not necessary requirements. Given the negative publicity associated with NINJA and LIAR loans, it would seem likely that Congress would limit lending institutions from continuing these practices.

Under the category of never missing an opportunity to miss an opportunity, U.S. Representative Barney Frank (D, Massachusetts) has returned to the scene of the calamity—with taxpayer money of course. He and U.S. Representative Anthony Weiner (D, New York) have sent a letter to the heads of Fannie and Freddie, exhorting them to lower lending standards for condo buyers. It helps to have a sense of humor.[20]

---

[19] "How the SEC Impedes the Growth of Small Business," Stephen A. Boyko, *The Yorktown Patriot*, Denver, Colorado, May 26, 2006.

[20] "Barney the Underwriter: Telling Fannie Mae to Take More Credit Risk. Now There's an Idea." *Wall Street Journal*, June 25, 2009.

PART THREE

Managing Change Results in a Net Benefit

TRANSFORMATIVE CHANGE

In Part I we examined the revenue side of the capital market equation from the perspective of a 34-year bull market. In Part II, we looked at the cost side of the capital market equation from the perspective of financial crises and stock market crashes. In this section, we will analyze the efficacy and efficiency of governance metrics outlined in financial regulatory reform proposed by the U.S. government.

This analysis adheres to a cardinal rule: Comprehensive governance should provide a net benefit for society. To this end, I echo the statement of Jamie Dimon, chairman and CEO of J.P. Morgan Chase & Company: "A reformed financial system must be in a position to create value for all of its stakeholders, customers, shareholders, employees, our communities, and for the economy as a whole."[1]

Capital market governance is in need of a significant transformation. U.S. Treasury Secretary Timothy Geithner and Lawrence Summers, director of the U.S. National Economic Council, made this point in a joint article, stating, "The financial system failed to perform its function as a reducer and distributor of risk. Instead, it magnified risks."

They went on to say the framework for financial regulation is riddled with gaps, weaknesses, and jurisdictional overlaps. It suffers from an outdated view of financial risk.[2]

If you want to revolutionize the capital market system, you must be willing to make real changes. The gaps (OTC derivatives), weaknesses (investment banking), and jurisdictional overlaps (where one credit card product offered by Chase was overseen by one regulator according to one set of standards, while a virtually identical product offered by a competitor would be overseen by a different regulator according to different standards[3]), identify the "what" questions. The outdated concept of financial risk is the "why."

---

[1] "A Unified Bank Regulator Is a Good Start," Jamie Dimon, *Wall Street Journal*, June 27, 2009.
[2] "A New Financial Foundation," Timothy Geithner and Lawrence Summers, *The Washington Post*, June 15, 2009.
[3] "A Unified Bank Regulator Is a Good Start," Jamie Dimon, *Wall Street Journal*, June 27, 2009.

I believe the "why"—the essential factor to randomness—to be the key to financial regulatory reform.

Fundamental to comprehensive governance is segmentation of the one-size-fits-all regulatory regime legacy. Segmentation should be done according to the randomness of the underlying economic environment of predictability, probability, and uncertainty. By extension, advocating for the segmentation of the regulatory scope is not incompatible with a single financial regulator.

In addressing "the soundness of the individual institutions but not the stability of the system as a whole,"[4] the suggested is that the whole is greater than the sum of its parts. Why? All the factors of randomness and uncertainty were not taken into account. Let's see what is needed to make real change.

For our purposes, **change** is the relationship between risk and uncertainty. A good dictionary defines "risk" as the chance of loss. Risk is probabilistic and thus presents foreseeable consequences, unlike "uncertainty," which is indeterminate and characterized by unforeseeable consequences.

"Uncertainty" is not a linear extension of "a riskier form of risk," but a separate and distinct concept. When uncertainty becomes risk, that's learning or innovation; you have greater control over your underlying economic environment. On the other hand, when risk becomes uncertainty, there is either confusion (too much information), or ambiguity (too little information). Should the uncertainty become unstable—as in New Orleans when the levies broke—you have chaos.

Change is difficult; it is management's number one problem. Change creates resistance due to loss of pay, power, prestige, and privilege.

Dimon's *Wall Street Journal* opinion piece echoes this: "Rewards have to track real, sustained, risk-adjusted performance. Golden parachutes, special contracts, and unreasonable perks must disappear."[5]

Motivation for change is a new job, a better job, or a different job.

The measures of change are scale, scope, span, and speed. **Scale** is a measure of size. Economies of scale hold that unit production cost decreases as the number of goods produced increases. The 2008 subprime stock market crash signifi-

---

[4] "A Unified Bank Regulator Is a Good Start," Jamie Dimon, *Wall Street Journal*, June 27, 2009.
[5] Ibid.

cantly reduced the scale of the capital market. NYSE issuer capitalization was down approximately $2 trillion in the first decade of the new century.[6]

Scope is the breadth or range of product offerings. The number of NYSE listings doubled from 1999 to 2009. Economies of scope hold that unit production costs decrease as variety of goods produced increase. The ability to cross-sell is an example. It is a key concept in determining whether the Bank of America-Merrill Lynch merger will be successful.

Span is the coordination of sequence and timing of production. Economies of span are achieved when the decreased transaction costs between stages of production and per-unit costs decline. Since 1974, more than 100 stock exchanges have come into existence globally.[7]

Speed is the rate of throughput. Economies of speed are achieved by using an asset to produce outputs at a higher rate of throughput. Discounting the increase in population, the number of years it takes a product to reach the critical mass of 50 million users has dropped significantly. As noted in Part I it took radio 38 years, and less than a century later, only four years for online retailing.

From a financial perspective, the period from 2000 to 2009 has seen the speed of throughput increase approximately four times, as measured in the NYSE daily volume.[8]

What is interesting is that "change" has changed. In the Industrial Age, change was binary—yes or no. A linear queuing theory drove change, and this theory had a first-move advantage.

In the Information Age, change was and continues to be information- and menu-driven—what we call "No-to-Know" or **N2K**. Change is now governed by wave and complexity theories. And unlike the Industrial Age, where usage depreciates an asset's value, in the Information Age usage appreciates the value of intellectual property.

Further, governance regimes are dynamic. They have changed over time. The NASDAQ and NYSE have gone from being markets to become financial firms with

---

[6] See on page 2.
[7] Stock Exchanges Worldwide Links, Aldas Kirvaitis, http://www.tdd.lt/slnews/Stock_Exchanges/Stock.Exchanges.html
[8] See on page 2.

transactional platforms. Government-Sponsored Enterprises (GSEs), such as Federal National Mortgage Corporation, also may become firms, while firms like Penn Central have become GSEs (Amtrak).

Finally, Wal-Mart has altered its governance structure to become a market by making huge investments in transactional enterprise software. This shift has enabled the retailer to reduce its inventory costs dramatically.

Entrepreneurs are commercial agents of change—conceptual problem solvers who fulfill unmet needs. They are transforming visionaries with a tenacious intent.

The Patron Saint of entrepreneurs is economist Joseph Schumpeter (1883-1950). He saw economic growth in terms innovation: new products, new processes, and new markets. He viewed the entrepreneur as a disturber of economic equilibrium and the primary cause of economic development. So why not take an entrepreneurial approach to reforming financial governance?

A SCIENTIFIC METHOD

To explain the scientific method former SEC Secretary Jonathan Katz[9] asked SEC staffers to use, we will look to Karl Raimund Popper (1902–1994) and his deductive-nomological (D-N) model.

Popper was an Austrian and British philosopher and professor at the London School of Economics. He is counted among the most influential scientific philosophers of the 20th century. Much of Popper's recent attention results from former student George Soros and his Reflexivity Theory.

Conceptually, Popper's D-N model is Euclidian geometry, with attendant axioms, postulates, and hypotheses, while Soros' Reflexivity Theory is calculus with its limit theories.

Popper wrote extensively on social and political philosophy. His vigorous defense of liberal democracies and principles of social criticism became the foundation for his vision for an "open society." Popper is best known for repudiating the classical scientific method through critical rationalism.[10]

---

[9] "Rules Are Not Sacred, Principles Are," Jonathan G. Katz, *Wall Street Journal*, August 8, 2006.
[10] Popper, Karl Raimund. *The Open Society and its Enemies: Hegel and Marx*, Vol. 2, Eighth Edition (Princeton University Press, Princeton, N.J., 2002).

Popper asserted that scientific laws could not be verified; they can only be falsified. Scientific laws can be tested by pairing the initial conditions with the final conditions. If they fail to conform to the scientific laws in question, that law is falsified.

Scientific laws are subject to two standards: predictability and the ability to replicate the results. Statements that cannot be proved false qualify as scientific. Therefore, one nonconforming instance may sufficiently invalidate the generalization in question. Conversely, no amounts of conforming instances sufficiently verify the generalization beyond any doubt.

Popper noted his model "illustrates philosopher Arthur Schopenhauer's remark that a solution of a problem often first looks like a paradox and later like a truism."[11] Yet his D-N model is a simple scheme of the scientific method consisting of three elements, three operations, and three logical observations.

An essential condition for the D-N model is that the content of the statements should exist in total isolation from related comments made about them.[12] This illustrates an interesting difference between physical science and social science experiments.

The Scientific Method Using Popper's D-N Model

The three elements are:
1. The initial condition
2. The final condition
3. Universally valid generalizations (scientific laws)

The three operations are:
1. Prediction: initial conditions combined with scientific laws
2. Explanation: final conditions combined with scientific laws
3. Testing: initial conditions compared to final conditions

The three logical observations are:
1. Symmetry between prediction and explanation (they are reversible, like multiplication and division)
2. Asymmetry between verification and falsification (one falsification can undo thousands of verifications)
3. The role of testing

---

[11] "Economic focus," Christina Romer, *The Economist*, June 20, 2009.
[12] Other such requirements are that the initial and final conditions should consist of facts, which lend themselves to scientific observation. Generalizations should have universal validity.

Scientific experiments are few in number, given the requirement for universal validity. However, scientific experiments can be tested an infinite number of times.

Conversely, social science experiments are many in number but difficult to replicate, given the human condition of learning. There also is the added condition that the experiment's statements should remain completely isolated from comments made about them. This requirement in particular is difficult to meet when experimenting with thinking participants.[13]

REFORM CONSIDERATIONS

The capability of capital market stakeholders notwithstanding, Popper's scientific method provides the analytic methodology to review *Financial Regulatory Reform: A New Foundation*, the U.S. Treasury's 88-page proposal released in 2009.

Known for his passion for financial arcane, Nobel prize-winning economist Even Merton Miller nonetheless characterized *Financial Regulatory Reform* as "dreadfully dull."[13] Put another way, the proposal suggests that the regulatory alphabet soup lose three letters—OTS (Office of Thrift Supervision)—and add four—CFPA (Consumer Financial Protection Agency).[14] In the end, the *federalis* yield a net benefit.

The introduction to the reform proposal[15] states that 2007 to 2009 brought the most severe financial crisis since the Great Depression. The roots of this crisis go back decades. Years without a serious economic recession bred complacency among financial intermediaries and investors. Financial crises had minimal impact on U.S. economic growth, which bred exaggerated expectations about the resilience of our financial markets and firms.

Rising asset prices, particularly in housing, hid weak credit underwriting standards and masked the growing leverage throughout the system. At some of our most sophisticated financial firms, risk management systems did not keep pace with the complexity of new financial products.

---

[13] Popper's scientific method was based on readings from George Soros's *The Alchemy of Finance; The New Paradigm for Financial Markets: The Credit Crisis of 2008 and What It Means; Open Society;* and *Underwriting Democracy.*

[14] "New Foundation, Walls Intact: A Much Trailed Financial Overhaul is a Curious Mix of Audacity and Timidity," *The Economist,* June 10, 2009.

[15] Ibid.

[16] *Financial Regulatory Reform,* Department of the U.S. Treasury, June 2009.

In a move to thwart the risky practices that plunged the country into economic crisis, President Barack Obama proposed a sweeping overhaul of financial regulations. This included placing limitations on major banking institutions; granting broad new powers to the Fed; steering consumers away from costly mortgages they could not afford; and other measures.

But how does the present proposal differ from SOX? After all, SOX was primarily a reaction to a number of major corporate and accounting scandals. It was billed as the cure-all for our then-financial ills. Yet the U.S. Treasury proposal acknowledges that the roots of the 2008 subprime crisis go back decades. Should not policymakers have addressed these issues when promulgating SOX?

SOX's regulatory efficacy is problematic. It mischaracterized the initial condition by prescribing remedies for corporate maladies to be instituted as market best practices. So is *Financial Regulatory Reform* a SOX mulligan?[16] Is it simply requesting additional resources—regulatory power, manpower, and budgetary power—to get a bigger hammer to drive a nail more effectively and efficiently?

Comprehensive reform should provide a societal net benefit. If it doesn't, then the mission should be redefined.

There are plenty of private-practice securities attorneys and accountants. Should the SEC staff focus on policy and assign private contractors to handle the majority of routine audits and investigatives? It seems to work for the military.

What justification is there for a government agency that does not produce a net benefit? Making the creation of a regulatory net benefit the goal will help staffers avoid group-think and subparagraph turf wars. This will in turn enable them to get ahead of the conceptual curve—a best practice from the consumerism approach. Thinking through cost constraints for the requisite changes in financial regulatory reform will improve the process.

A critical matter related to the notion that benefits must be greater than the added cost of the regulatory burden is that new regulation must be proportionate. Regulation is a negative operational tax: "Thou shall not—except for." Every practitioner tries to create an "except for" category to gain a competitive advantage.

---

[17] A golf term for a penalty-free redo.

Regulators do about as good a job as they can with the growing structural difficulties of trying to govern randomness within a one-size-fits-all regime. It is similar to having one driving manual for the United States and the United Kingdom, even though we drive on different sides of the road. But what industry thermostat will be used to determine if a too hot, too cold, just right Goldilocks type of reform works?

Christina Romer, chair of Council of Economic Advisors in the Obama administration and Great Depression scholar, advises against over control and over regulation. Instead, she says today's policymakers must learn from the errors that prolonged the depression, offering the second downturn of 1937 as a cautionary tale.[18]

"The urge to declare victory and get back to normal policy after an economic crisis is strong," Romer wrote in a June 18, 2009, guest column for *The Economist*. "That urge needs to be resisted until the economy is again approaching full employment. Financial crises, in particular, tend to leave scars that make financial institutions, households, and firms behave differently."

Her analysis is simple: To become austere in the immediate future would surely set back the recovery and risk a 1937-like recession within-a-recession.[19]

APPLYING POPPER'S MODEL TO REGULATION

Popper's Model Applied to Regulation on page 68 illustrates how Popper's D-N model can help us visualize our scientific regulatory experiment.

In the model's elements category, we identify the initial condition, final condition, and universally valid generalizations. The initial condition is comprised of the financial crises and stock market crashes discussed in Part I and listed again in the model on page 68.

The final condition consists of recommendations outlined in *Financial Regulatory Reform*:

1. Promote robust supervision and regulation of financial firms.
2. Establish comprehensive regulation of financial markets.
3. Protect consumers and investors from financial abuse.
4. Provide the government with the tools it needs to manage financial crises.
5. Raise international regulatory standards and improve international cooperation.

---

[18] "Economic Focus," Christina Romer, *The Economist*, June 20, 2009.
[19] Ibid.

Popper's Model Applied to Regulation

Initial Condition	Universally Valid Generalizations	Final Conditions
Herstatt Bank of Cologne crisis LTCM crisis Enron crisis Madoff Ponzi-scheme crisis Crash of 1987 Savings & Loan crash Dot-com crash 2008 subprime crash	Results in command side of the governance model	Recommendations from U.S. Treasury 1. Promote Robust Supervision/ Regulation of Firms 2. Establish Comprehensive Regulation of Markets 3. Protect Consumers/Investors from Abuse 4. Provide Government with Tools to Manage Crises 5. Raise International Regulatory Standards; Improve International Cooperation

In our experiment, we discover that universally valid generalizations are the command side of the governance model, outlining standards and rules. Capital market governance is a reflexive process involving commands and incentives.[20]

As illustrated in the **Normative Governance Model** on page 69, regulators create governance regimes by choosing appropriate commands for the incentives available in the economy. Commands and incentives are different sides of a governance equation for a given level of economic activity.

The sides of the model are also self-referential; one cannot be discussed in the absence of the other. As you will see in the model on page 69, command costs attendant to shareholder rights, enforcement activities, and efforts to limit rent-seeking schemes correspond with incentives derived from shareholder responsibilities (to be good financial shoppers in terms of price discovery and sales practices) and opportunities for free riding. This reflexive, open process allows market realities to evolve.

The command side of the **Normative Governance Model** is comprised of shareholder rights, enforcement activities, and rent-seeking components. Shareholder rights are a composite of principles and rules. **Principles** are prospective

---

[20] "Fit Regulation to Market Reality," Stephen A. Boyko, *SFO Magazine* April 2009.

Normative Governance Model

```
                          Normative
                       Governance Model
           ┌──────────────────┴──────────────────┐
        Commands                              Incentives
    ┌───────┬────────┬────────┐          ┌────────┬────────┐
Shareholder Enforcement Rent Seeking:   Rent Seeking:  Free Riding:
  Rights                 public            public        private
                       opportunism      opportunism   opportunism

- Principles  - Commitment  - Controlled    - Pricing    - Non-production
- Rules       - Capacity      Externalities - Practices    of public goods
              - Capability  - Unappropriated             - Disproportionate
              - Condition     Resources                    benefits
```

societal policies that define industry effectiveness in terms of the right things to do. The FLITE model of fairness, liquidity, integration, transparency, and efficiency represents such principles. Principles are defined in terms of mass, or the number of people affected by the command, and **materiality**, indicating the relative importance of the command.

Rules, on the other hand, are the retrospective arrangement of best-practice procedures that define operational efficiency in terms of doing things correctly. They are industry proscriptions that explicitly delineate organizational limits in terms of gravitas and granularity. **Gravitas** is the seriousness of a violation, as measured by the amount of a fine or punishment. **Granularity** is the degree of precision required for compliance.

For example, liquidity exists when there are sufficient buyers and sellers to consummate transactions at prices reasonably related to quoted market prices. It is a function of time, volatility, depth, breadth, and the resiliency of the marketplace.

The **Net Capital Rule** is based on a liquidation concept requirement that broker-dealers have sufficient capital. Asset type, aggregate level of reserves, and the ratio of liabilities to assets combine to determine whether a broker-dealer has sufficient capital. To satisfy the Net Capital Rule, all three must be at levels that allow the broker-dealer in question to continuously meet all outstanding liabilities.

Enforcement is the tactical application of regulatory principles and rules. The SEC's mission is to "protect investors; maintain fair, orderly, and efficient markets; and facilitate capital formation." The Division of Enforcement's role is to assist the SEC in executing its law enforcement function by recommending the investigation of securities law violations. In addition, the Division of Enforcement also can recommend that the commission bring civil actions in a federal court or before an administrative law judge and/or prosecute these cases on behalf of the SEC.

Rent seekers are economic actors who manipulate the economic and/or legal environment. The term is generally associated with government regulation and misuse of governmental authority. Rent seekers claiming to "protect investors" extract uncompensated value from unappropriated resources without making a commensurate contribution. If Congress contemplates forcing financial executives and directors to pay clawbacks (penalty repayments) because their fiduciary responsibility was questionable or lacking, should not Congress apply that same standard to the SEC staff?

The SEC currently finds itself in a difficult position, due to a greater demand for the regulatory services required by complex investments in global markets. Like Citigroup, the SEC can no longer effectively manage with a one-size-fits-all regulatory regime. If you can't cross-sell, you can't cross-regulate.

Efficient utilization of regulatory resources requires a modification of the commission's central organizational structure and the legacy practices tied to Neoclassical economics and deterministic legal and accounting frameworks.

Markets are dynamic, nonlinear systems that place exponential demands on regulatory services. This conflicts with the SEC's linear budgetary ability to supply regulatory resources. The SEC faces a Hobson's choice:[21] Constrain enforcement efforts—and risk its Madoff-type errors of omission; or fall behind the regulatory curve and risk revisiting subprime-type errors of commission.

Compensating for this regulatory resource shortage requires investors to become qualified. Without a proportionate increase in investors' financial knowledge, regulation merely "dumbs-down" the consumer base at the expense of market efficiency.

Many Madoff investors now realize that "protection" is a racket— much to their chagrin. So-called protection creates a moral hazard, where unsophisticated investors receive a regulatory subsidy to expand the scale, scope, and span of their

---

[21] A choice between something or nothing.

investment activity. Just as taking a driver's education course reduces the student's auto insurance costs, investors who become financially sophisticated and educate themselves reduce the cost of compliance. Qualifying investor suitability then enables the SEC to become more efficient by substituting intellectual capital for financial capital.

USING SOX TO DEMONSTRATE POPPER'S THREE OPERATIONS

A review of SOX illustrates the three operations: prediction, explanation, and testing. Because there is an asymmetrical relationship between verification and falsification, these operations are negatively framed in terms of mischaracterization, misapplication, and misspecification.

Prediction combines the initial conditions with universally valid generalizations. SOX mischaracterized the initial condition, resulting in a disproportionate level of commands to incentives. Regulatory proposals designed for top-tier market and determinate, positive cash-flow enterprises are disproportionate when applied to indeterminate, negative cash-flow small- and medium-sized enterprises (SMEs).

Two former Fed chairmen defend this top-tier perspective. Paul Volcker (1979 to 1987) and Arthur Levitt (1993 to 2001) justified the added cost of SOX by noting that spending almost $5 million each to implement each SOX control and an additional $1.5 million annually to maintain those control structures is not too for a multibillion-dollar international company to pay when compared with what investors can lose.[22]

But what about marginalized SMEs that cannot afford such added costs? Do we continue to treat SMEs the same as large corporations?

To do so is to create a case of mixing apples and oranges. The effect of the one-size-fits-all regulatory regime has been to create an asymmetrical burden upon SMEs by increasing the cost of compliance and lowering their market capitalization. To paraphrase Hernando DeSoto's insight from *The Mystery of Capital-*

---

[22] Gitlow, Abraham Leo. *Corruption in Corporate America: Who is Responsible? Who Will Protect the Public Interest?*, (University Press of America, Lanham, Maryland, 2005) Appendices I and II, p. 133 and p. 155-156.

ism, it's not that SMEs broke rules created for large-cap issuers; it's that SOX-type rules broke SMEs.

Popper's explanation operation combines final conditions with universally valid generalizations. SOX is a classic example of misapplying retrospective rules to plan. Passed in the aftermath of the Enron and WorldCom accounting irregularities, SOX has raised the cost of compliance without offering much in the way of long-term solutions for correcting the accounting problems that befell Bear Sterns, Lehman Bros., American International Group, and Merrill Lynch.

A study by law firm Foley & Lardner found that since Fiscal Year 2003, companies of all sizes have experienced a significant increase in SOX compliance costs, with total fees paid to auditors increasing 59% for all companies analyzed. Further, the increase was approximately 50% greater for small-cap issuers, when compared with large-cap issuers.[23]

The testing operation of Popper's model compares initial conditions to final conditions. SOX mischaracterized commercial activity by equating risk with uncertainty. SOX is a large operational tax on wealth creation and innovation that gives rise to unintended consequences. The more top-tier regulatory commands strive for predictive capability, the more imprecise the management of SME commercial activity, due to transactional transference to market externalities (i.e., AIM).

The more commands add costs to the SME market, the greater the incentive to either go private, underground, and/or offshore to conduct business. This in turn causes the U.S. capital market to become less transparent, less innovative, and less productive. Given these results, the efficacy of SOX appears problematic.

Now let's review of *Financial Regulatory Reform*. I have excerpted information from the report, as indicated, followed by my own comments. For your benefit, I have prefaced each with a synopsis of the recommendation, along with key supporting sections.[24]

---

[23] "The Cost of Being Public in the Era of Sarbanes-Oxley," presented by Thomas E. Hartman, August 2, 2007, Foley & Lardner LLP.

[24] The U.S. Treasury makes the full text of the report available for download on its website: www.financialstability.gov/docs.

RECOMMENDATION 1: PROMOTE ROBUST SUPERVISION AND REGULATION OF FINANCIAL FIRMS

Financial Regulatory Reform *states that in the years leading up to the current financial crisis, risks built up dangerously in our financial system.*

Comment: Policymakers must broaden their horizons to see beyond the concept of risk and begin to understand fully the concept of randomness.

Randomness is a process describing the probability of a factor being chosen within a range of 0%, or indeterminate, to 100%, or predictive certainty. Recognition and attendant disclosure of the prevailing economic environment is the foundation that drives governance for indeterminate and determinate regimes.

Innovation is the hallmark of capital markets, yet innovative solutions for global markets create greater complexity.[25] Complexity begets uncertainty, as innovative financial products evolve from earlier, simpler versions to address heretofore uncertain and unforeseeable circumstances.

Paraphrasing economist Frank H. Knight's *Risk, Uncertainty, and Profit,* New York University economist Nouriel Roubini distinguishes between the two: "Risk and uncertainty: The former can be priced by financial markets while the latter cannot. ... Indeed, for many reasons, the current market panic has more to do with unpriceable uncertainty rather than measurable risk."[26]

For markets to be robust and innovative, the investment environment must provide opportunities that arise from "uncertainty." If all segments of the capital markets were as probabilistic and deterministic as Financial Regulatory Reform suggests, problems with deus ex machina enterprises such as Long Term Capital Management (LTCM) would be unlikely.[27]

---

[25] Peters, Edgar. *Complexity, Risk, and Financial Markets* (Wiley: N.Y., 1999) p. 19.
[26] "Current Market Turmoil: Non-Priceable Knightian 'Uncertainty' Rather than Priceable Market 'Risk,'" Nouriel Roubini's *Global EconoMonitor,* August 15, 2007.
[27] "Too Big to Fail: Long Term Capital Management and the Federal Reserve," Kevin Dowd, Briefing Paper No. 53, *The Cato Institute,* September 23, 1999. In September 1998, the Fed organized a rescue of LTCM, a large and prominent hedge fund. The Fed intervened because it was concerned about possible dire consequences for world financial markets if it allowed the hedge fund to fail. Dowd argues that the Fed's intervention was misguided and unnecessary. LTCM would not have failed, and the Fed's concerns about the effects of its failure on financial markets were exaggerated. In the short run, the Fed's intervention helped the shareholders and managers of LTCM get better exit deals.

> *In* Financial Regulatory Reform, *the U.S. Treasury acknowledges that its supervisory framework was not equipped to handle a financial dislocation of the magnitude of the 2008 subprime crash. To be sure, nearly all of the largest, most interconnected, and most highly leveraged financial firms in the country were subject to some form of supervision and regulation by a federal government agency. But those forms of supervision and regulation proved inadequate.*

Comment: The U.S. capital market regulatory structure is a hierarchical command-and-control process similar to the Soviet Union's *Gosplan*. It lacked the information system to restructure and, therefore, was unable to address effectively the complexities required by the Information Age.

Similarly, U.S. regulators are not prepared to meet the greater demand for resources required by global mass markets and the greater complexity required by innovative products. The SEC can no longer effectively govern with a deterministic, one-size-fits-all regulatory regime. Robust markets create an exponential demand for compliance in comparison to the SEC's linear ability to supply regulatory resources.

This creates a no-win choice for the SEC; either constrain market dynamics and commit errors of omission, (i.e., sending business offshore to the AIM) or fall behind the compliance curve and commit errors of commission (i.e., Madoff).

As a former regulator, I believe current regulators get a bum rap in all of this. They are now in the position of practitioner, in that they are held accountable for market uncertainties that are not supported by their deterministic metrics.

They are being forced to play out of position. If we have a great left-handed baseball player, why would we play him on third base instead of first? Regulators do certain things very well. They regulate the deterministic markets very well. This is in large part due to staffers being trained in the deterministic disciplines of law, accounting, and Neoclassical economics. How many were trained to govern uncertainty?

> Financial Regulatory Reform *finds that on a systemic basis, regulators did not take into account the harm that large, interconnected, and highly leveraged institutions could inflict on the financial system.*

Comment: It is said that a picture is worth a thousand words. As a result, I offer **Reduced to Ponzi Borrowers** on page 75 to illustrate.

You might study this figure and believe it to be a well hedged position, but excessive leverage and related restructuring costs do not appear to result in a loss position for any long-term investor beyond three months.

As the graph indicates, this situation has reduced such highly leveraged institutions to "Ponzi borrowers." They borrow based on the belief that the appreciation of the value of the underlying asset will be sufficient to refinance the debt. The Ponzi borrower could not make sufficient payments on interest or principal with the cash flow from investments. Only a rapidly appreciating asset value can keep the Ponzi borrower afloat.[28]

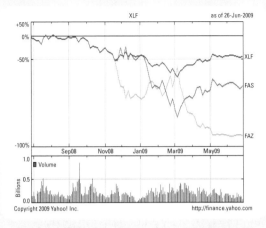

Reduced to 'Ponzi Borrowers'

The above shows Direxion Daily Financial Bull 3X Shares Exchange Trade Funds (NYSE symbol: FAS), Direxion Daily Financial Bear 3X Shares Exchange Trade Funds (NYSE symbol: FAZ), and Financial Select Sector SPDR (XLF). This chart serves as a proxy for highly leveraged institutions that engaged in complex, subprime products. They are reduced to being, as Minsky notes, "Ponzi borrowers" who borrow based on the belief that the appreciation of the value of the underlying asset will be sufficient to refinance the debt.

To overcome these governance shortcomings, Financial Regulatory Reform proposes the creation of a Financial Services Oversight Council, run by the U.S. Treasury, to help fill gaps in supervision; facilitate coordination of policy and resolution of disputes; and identify emerging risks in firms and market activities. This council would include the heads of the principal federal financial regulators and would maintain a permanent staff at the U.S. Treasury.

---

[28] Kindleberger, Charles and Robert Aliber. *Manias, Panics, and Crashes*, Fifth Edition, (John Wiley & Sons Inc., New York, N.Y.) p. 27-28.

Comment: I believe this could go a long way toward enhancing the flow and exchange of information, but the "why" remains unanswered. *Financial Regulatory Reform* treats the symptoms, not the cause. To assure effective capital market governance, risk management must evolve to respond to randomness, thereby ensuring information correlation for predictable, probabilistic, and uncertain underlying economic environments.

> Financial Regulatory Reform *states that authority for supervision and regulation of Tier 1 Financial Holding Companies (FHCs) be vested in the Federal Reserve Board, which is by statute the consolidated supervisor and regulator of all bank holding companies today. As a result of changes in corporate structure during the current crisis, the Federal Reserve already supervises and regulates all major U.S. commercial and investment banks on a firm-wide basis. The Federal Reserve has by far the most experience and resources to handle consolidated supervision and regulation of Tier 1 FHCs.*
>
> Key to Financial Regulatory Reform *is improving coordination to reduce the threat of systemic risk. The U.S. Treasury recommends legislation to specify factors that the Federal Reserve must consider when determining whether an individual financial firm poses a threat to financial stability. Those proposed factors include:*
> 1. *The impact the firm's failure would have on the financial system and the economy;*
> 2. *The firm's combination of size, leverage (including off-balance sheet exposures), and degree of reliance on short-term funding;*
> 3. *The firm's criticality as a source of credit for households, businesses, and state and local governments and as a source of liquidity for the financial system.*

Comment: This has the potential to develop into a robust, three-dimensional governance model with a quantitative X-axis (minimum capital requirement), qualitative Y-axis (liquidity), and relationship Z-axis (degree of connectedness). More on three-dimensional governance models later. Kudos to the policymakers for getting ahead of the curve.

RECOMMENDATION 2: ESTABLISH COMPREHENSIVE REGULATION OF FINANCIAL MARKETS

> Financial Regulatory Reform *states that Tier 1 FHCs should be subject to heightened supervision and regulation because of the greater risks their potential failure would pose to the financial system. At the same time, given the important role of Tier 1 FHCs in the financial system and the economy, setting their prudential standards too high could constrain long-term financial and economic growth. Therefore, the Federal Reserve, in consultation with the Financial Services Oversight Council, should set prudential standards for Tier 1 FHCs to maximize financial stability at the lowest cost to long-term financial and economic growth.*

Comment: Comprehensive governance regimes choose appropriate commands for the incentive set available in the economy.[29] This balances incentives derived from shareholder responsibilities with command costs attendant to shareholder rights.

In consulting the **Governance Randomness Matrix** on page 78, we note that the pricing construct holds cash flow as the line between risk and uncertainty. There are the dual benchmarks of positive cash flow and negative cash flow in an indeterminate economic environment. Companies with a negative cash flow emphasize tactical management of their burn rate to survive, while companies with positive cash flow emphasize strategic management of the enterprise's value proposition.

The sales practice construct involves the reflexive interaction of sellers and buyers. Economists hold that for every seller there is a buyer, and vice versa. While this borders on the tautological, it is germane from a financial market perspective whether the seller or the buyer initiated the transaction.

Commercial practice holds that the party who initiates the transaction is most likely to set the terms and conditions of commercial engagement, determining whether the good was bought on an unsolicited basis or sold on a solicited basis.

As illustrated in the **Governance Randomness Matrix**, formulaically predictable investments, such as U.S. Treasury Bonds, are *bought* and valued on a mark-to-market basis in a determinate economic environment. Money market instruments require decision-making tasks, with both the state of the market and the probability of issuer cash flow distributions known.

---

[29] "Best Fit for Best Practice Governance," Stephen A. Boyko, *SFO Magazine*, January 2009.

Governance Randomness Matrix

PRICING PRACTICES	POSITIVE CASH FLOW MARK-TO-MARKET DETERMINATE	NEGATIVE CASH FLOW MARK-TO-MODEL INDETERMINATE
Stocks that are bought	Formulaic Predictability Money Market Knowable Knowns	Unsure M&A Unknowable Knowns
Stocks that are sold	Probabilistic IPOs Knowable Unknowns	Uncertain Private Placements Unknowable Unknowns

This matrix analyzes the balancing of the market's invisible hand with the government's iron fist. The pricing construct holds cash flow as the line that demarcates risk from uncertainty. It has binary benchmarks consisting of positive cash flow that is marked-to-market in a determinate economic environment, and negative cash flow that is marked-to-model in an indeterminate economic environment. Companies with a negative cash flow emphasize tactical management of their "burn rate" to survive, while companies with positive cash flow emphasize strategic management of the enterprise's value proposition. Unlike positive cash flow companies that employ risk management techniques to maximize value in a probabilistic environment, negative cash flow companies seek to minimize dilution from their burn rate by selling stock and product in an uncertain environment until their critical event occurs (e.g., FDA patent approval).

Probabilistic investments that are *sold* are valued on a mark-to-market basis in a determinate economic environment. Investments like IPOs require decision making where the state of market is known but the cash flow expected value is unknown.

Negative cash flow investments that are marked-to-model in an indeterminate economic environment with *bought* sales practices tend to have unsure valuations. Transactions such as an "acquisition" or "going private" require decision-making procedures where the state of market is unknown but the probabilistic expected value of enterprise cash flow is known.

Negative cash flow investments that are marked-to-model in an indeterminate economic environment with *sold* sales practices have uncertain valuations. Investments such as a private placement in a new enterprise or credit swap derivatives require decision-making procedures where the state of market and the probabilistic expected value of enterprise cash flow distributions are unknown.

Financial Regulatory Reform *proposes to enhance the Federal Reserve's authority over market infrastructure to reduce the potential for contagion among financial firms and markets.*

The current financial crisis occurred after a long and remarkable period of growth and innovation in U.S. financial markets. New financial instruments allowed credit risks to be spread widely, enabling investors to diversify their portfolios in new ways while enabling banks to shed exposures that had once stayed on their balance sheets.

However, instead of appropriately distributing risks, this process often concentrated risk in opaque and complex ways. Innovations occurred too rapidly for many financial institutions' risk management systems; for the market infrastructure, which consists of payment, clearing, and settlement systems; and for the nation's financial supervisors.

Investors became overly reliant on credit-rating agencies. Credit ratings often failed to describe accurately the risk of rated products. In each case, lack of transparency prevented market participants from understanding the full nature of the risks and uncertainties inherent in the investment.

The build-up of risk in the OTC derivatives markets, which were thought to disperse risk to those most able to bear it, eventually contaminated the financial sector during the crisis. Financial Regulatory Reform brings the markets for all OTC derivatives and asset-backed securities into a coherent and coordinated regulatory framework that requires transparency and improves market discipline. A strengthening of prudential regulation of all dealers in the OTC derivative markets also is proposed, along with requiring that all standardized OTC derivative transactions be executed in regulated and transparent venues and cleared through regulated, central counter-parties. Doing so will reduce the systemic risk in these markets.

Lastly, the proposal seeks to harmonize the statutory and regulatory regimes for futures and securities. While differences exist between securities and futures markets, many differences in regulation between the markets may no longer be justified. In particular, the growth of derivatives markets and the introduction of new derivative instruments have highlighted the need for addressing gaps and inconsistencies in the regulation of these products by the U.S. Commodity Futures Trading Commission and SEC.

Comment: Once again the symptoms are addressed while the underlying causes help the disease continue to spread. The cure is to segment the randomness of the one-size-fits-all regulatory regime.

As you'll note in the **Governance Segmentation Matrix** on page 80, the combination of retrospective time perspective and determinate economic environment

Governance Segmentation Martrix

TIME FRAME RANDOMNESS	RETROSPECTIVE	PROSPECTIVE
Determinate	Rules Codified Best Practices	Pillared-Risk Outcome Assessment
Indeterminate	Relationships Lineage / Political	Principles Prudential Norms

The timeframe construct of the Governance Segmentation Matrix's has binary benchmarks consisting of retrospective and prospective points of view. The matrix's randomness construct has binary benchmarks consisting of determinate and indeterminate economic environments.

tend toward rules-based governance. While rules-based systems give specific guidance, they can sometimes be too rigid, leading to a "tick-the-box" approach. A rules-based system works well in deterministic economic environments with mature companies.

Meanwhile, prospective time perspective and determinate economic environment suggest a pillared-risk outcome assessment regime similar to the Basel approach.[30] Pillared-risk outcome assessments identify, characterize, and understand risk, relative to alternative strategies. Cost-benefit analysis, assessment of risk tolerance, and quantification of preference outcomes are often involved in this decision-making process. Outcome assessment regimes work well in a deterministic economic environment with growth companies.

Retrospective time perspective linked with indeterminate economic environment is conducive to a relationship-based governance regime like the London Stock Exchange's AIM. AIM has a wide community of expert advisers, including Nominated Advisers (nicknamed "Nomads"), brokers, accountants, lawyers, and public relations firms. A relationship-based system has lower fixed costs but higher variable costs, because trading is on a small scale among interested

---

[30] The capital regime used by regulators for the world's largest banks.

practitioners. Relationship governance works well in an indeterminate economic environment with early-stage public companies.

Governance Segmentation Matrix also shows that the combination of prospective time perspective and indeterminate economic environment favor a principles-based system organized around a relatively small number of prudential norms. The advantage of a principles-based system is its flexibility and sensibility in dealing with new or special situations. Principle-based systems work well in an indeterminate economic environment with entrepreneurial enterprises.

Governance of today's global capital markets requires a segmented, multifaceted approach that functions in a three-dimensional model (vertical firms, horizontal markets, and perpendicular neural networks for integration). Such governance plans recognize and adapt to risk vs. uncertainty economic environments and organize market interaction effectively among investors, issuers, and intermediaries.

If policymakers propose changes in capital market governance, there needs to be real and fundamental change, not bureaucratic posturing.

Too often reformers pour gasoline on the fire by raising regulatory standards ill correlated to the problem(s) at hand; remember SOX was the reform to end all reforms.

As I noted in an article co-authored with Aron Gottesman of Pace University, "Reformers can behave reactively, suggestive of bounded rationality; place too much emphasis on realized events instead of the universe of potential events; and limit their problem-solving focus to realized effects that results from confirmation bias and group-think."[31]

The problem is the monopolistic nature of the legacy, one-size-fits-all regulatory model, which thwarts the natural tendency of markets to segment. As law professors S.J. Choi and A.C. Pritchard argue, while markets correct themselves, regulators resist corrections.[32]

Vertical, command-and-control regulatory metrics immobilize capital by limiting alternative solutions for the horizontal market. Such biases are exacerbat-

---

[31] "Small is Beautiful," Stephen A. Boyko and Aron A. Gottesman, *The National Interest*, No. 77, Fall 2004.
[32] Choi, Stephen J., and A.C. Pritchard. *Securities Regulation: Cases and Analysis*, Second Edition (Foundation Press, 2008) p. 1.

ed by a political system that requires immediate solutions in reaction to publicized crises, as illustrated by the recent home loan credit meltdown and the resultant TARP. As a nation, it has cost taxpayers nearly a trillion dollars to recognize the need for regulatory change—so far.

This book argues that as markets become more robust, consumers seek financial instruments tailored—with increasing precision—to their needs. Markets tend to segment into different groups of stakeholders that respond to material information with a high degree of affinity that is measurable and accessible through different regulatory protocols. Necessary for operational efficiency of robust markets is transparency, which reveals the distinction between the determinate and indeterminate economic environments.

RECOMMENDATION 3: PROTECT CONSUMERS AND INVESTORS FROM FINANCIAL ABUSE

According to Financial Regulatory Reform, *Congress, the presidential administration, and financial regulators took significant measures to address some of the most obvious inadequacies in our consumer-protection framework. These steps have focused on two very important, product markets: credit cards and mortgages. We need comprehensive reform.*

For that reason, Financial Regulatory Reform *proposes the creation of Consumer Financial Protection Agency (CFPA), a single regulatory agency with the authority and accountability to ensure consumer protection regulations are written fairly and enforced vigorously.*

Consumer protection is a critical foundation the U.S. financial system. It gives the public confidence that financial markets are fair and enables policymakers and regulators to maintain stability in regulation. To this end, the SEC is to protect investors, improve disclosure, raise standards, and increase enforcement.

Comment: This sound nice, but consumer protection correlates directly with consumer knowledge. Until consumers have skin in the game in the form of either intellectual and/or financial capital, investor protection is a promise that can't be kept. Whether that promise of protection is uttered by Don Corleone in *The Godfather* or "Don" Columbia Law School, protection is a racket. When is the last time an aggrieved customer got a check from a regulator? Customer confidence begins with insuring, ensuring, and assuring that there is a sufficient capital cushion to clear all trades.

No longer can a fail-safe governance system be provided that is based only on financial capacity, like the accredited investor concept. We need to qualify investor capabilities.

When speaking about this concept, critics say that you can't qualify everyone; it is a monumental task. My response is that most of us have a driver's license. Yet few of us have a Class-A commercial driver's license, which would clear us to drive 18-wheelers. In other words, we qualify people for important tasks every day—so people can *protect themselves.* Substituting "too dumb to succeed" for "too big to fail" is not a commercially viable strategy. Ask General Motors!

The same concept holds for financial responsibility. Everybody talks about shareholder rights. You cannot have shareholder rights that are disproportionate to shareholder responsibilities; otherwise, you create subsidies. It is either rent seeking on the part of the public sector or free riding on the part of the private sector.

Disproportionate governance creates subsidies. It is similar to price-support subsidies for dairy farmers. With controls, you get black markets and/or supply shortages. Conversely, with subsidies you get oversupply and excess capacity of products. Subsidies are not a viable market solution. Absent proportionality, your regulatory services are priced with an average cost model, which acts as a function of an unappropriated surplus in the name of investor protection.

There is no better example of rent-seeking subsidies than the U.S. Treasury's proposal that CFPA create a series of recommendations for legislation, regulations, and administrative measures, which it hopes will reform consumer protection based on principles of transparency, simplicity, fairness, accountability, and access for all.

> Financial Regulatory Reform *goes on to propose transparency in all mandatory disclosure forms, so they will be clear, simple, and concise.*

Comment: Bravo for apple pie! But weren't mutual fund prospectuses also supposed to be clear, simple, and concise? Does this proposal mean the CFPA should make judgments about which risks and costs should be highlighted and which need not be? And which staffer will assume the liability?

This is similar to letting the referee shoot the free throw at the end of the game to determine the victor.

> Financial Regulatory Reform *states that consumers should verify their ability to understand and use disclosure forms with qualitative and statistical tests.*

Comment: Is there a distance-learning center at which consumers can be educated so they can achieve a minimum threshold? (And what happened to "clear, simple, and concise"?) There must be an educational component to enhance shareholder responsibilities.

> Financial Regulatory Reform *also highlights simplicity. Even if disclosures are fully tested and all communications are properly balanced, product complexity itself can lead consumers to make costly errors. A careful regulatory approach can tilt the scales in favor of simpler, less risky products while preserving choice and innovation.*

Comment: Complex for whom? Isn't this the difference between a mass market, with products that are bought, as compared to a niche market, with products that are sold?

Much of this is a business decision—deciding whether your business should have a marketing department or a sales force. There are two types of products: those that are sold, and those that are bought.

Firms underwrite innovative products that must be sold. They refine transactional processes through "intermediation" and "infomediation." As products/services mature, they can be bought and easily integrated into market. The invisible hand of the market creates wealth by reflexively perfecting the transactional processes and products of target and reverse markets.

Goods and services that are sold in target markets are regarded as "works in progress." They require firm sponsorship in order for transactions to be completed. A reverse market (i.e., e*retailing) is where the customer initiates a transaction with a vendor. Goods and services that are bought in reverse markets are self-selected by consumers. They are complete, with respect to both product information and market infrastructure.

> *Where efforts to improve transparency and simplicity prove inadequate to prevent unfair treatment and abuse,* Financial Regulatory Reform *proposes granting the CFPA authority to place tailored restrictions on product terms and provider prac-*

tices—if the benefits outweigh the costs. Moreover, the report proposes authorizing the CFPA to impose appropriate duties of care on financial intermediaries.

Comment: There is a reason this book it titled *We're All Screwed*. Fair or unfair is in the eye of the stakeholder. Regulation does not stop commercial competition, nor can it render it "more fair." Once the market validates a critical level of demand, regulation can only determine how much something costs and where it can be acquired.

Is it fair for an entrepreneur to have his innovative "black swan" product judged by someone other than the market? Was Jack Welch's "GE Six Sigma" concept an unfair advantage? How would you like to fly in a plane that had only a One Sigma standard?

If someone has a comparative advantage—or whose core competencies are naturally superior—does that person have to compete with a handicap? Would anyone go to watch Michael Jordan play basketball if he had to wear gloves and galoshes to make it "more fair" for the other players? How much of a weight handicap would Secretariat have to carry to make the race "more equal"? And if that could be determined, would spectators have been deprived of that marvelous stretch run to break the Belmont record?

The "fairness doctrine" is blatant commercial censorship. What are the commercial qualifications of the judges? More importantly, this could be the entrepreneur's "black swan" event; is it to be stored in some government warehouse next to the Ark of the Covenant?

Fairness doctrines create mediocrity, not a meritocracy.

To improve access, Financial Regulatory Reform *proposes the CFPA enforce fair lending laws and the Community Reinvestment Act and otherwise seek to ensure that underserved consumers and communities have access to prudent financial services, lending, and investment.*

Comment: How does the CFPA reconcile universal access with business judgment? At some level of universal subsidized access, can a shareholder claim a nonprofit tax exemption? Was the term "subprime" a misnomer? Should loan applications be priced on the margin, like United Parcel Service, or on the average, like the U.S. Postal Service?

The U.S. Treasury's mindset lacks the real world context necessary to form consumer best practices.

RECOMMENDATION 4: PROVIDE THE GOVERNMENT WITH THE TOOLS IT NEEDS TO MANAGE FINANCIAL CRISES

> *Since 2007, the financial system has been threatened by the failure or near failure of some of the largest and most interconnected financial firms. The nation's current system already has strong procedures and expertise for handling the bank failures, but when a bank holding company or other non-bank financial firm is in severe distress, there are currently only two options: obtain outside capital or file for bankruptcy. In most economic climates, these suitable options will not affect greater financial stability.*
>
> *However, in stressed conditions it may prove difficult for distressed institutions to raise sufficient private capital. Thus, if a large, interconnected bank holding company or other non-bank financial firm nears failure during a financial crisis, there are only two untenable options: obtain emergency funding from the U.S. government, as in the case of AIG, or file for bankruptcy, as in the case of Lehman Brothers. Neither of these options is acceptable for managing the resolution of the firm efficiently and effectively in a manner that limits the systemic risk with the least cost to the taxpayer.*
>
> Financial Regulatory Reform *proposes a new authority modeled on the existing authority of the FDIC, which would allow the government to address the potential failure of a bank holding company or other non-bank financial firm when the stability of the financial system is at risk.*
>
> *To improve accountability in the use of other crisis tools, the report also proposes that the Federal Reserve Board receives prior written approval from the secretary of the treasury for emergency lending under its "unusual and exigent circumstances" authority.*

Comment: When contingency planning for the "unknowable, unknown" event, does the model drive the decision (deterministic conditionality) or merely provide guidelines for a resolution regime for failing firms?

Notwithstanding all the projections as to how smoothly things will function in the future, given the implementation of the U.S. Treasury's proposals, it appears the treasury wants "CYA"[33] justification if it has to take control.

---

[33] An acronym for "cover your ass"—the cardinal rule of bureaucrats. They have amazing survival instincts. The U.S. Treasury proposal testifies to this.

Similar arguments were made for SOX—new toys, same old arguments. Given the comprehensive nature of SOX, why in just the few years since its adoption were there governance gaps? Regulatory overlaps? Enforcement naps? It is the Golden Rule,[34] and the treasury has the biggest checkbook.

What I find interesting is that this section of the treasury report deals with contingency planning for "unusual and exigent circumstances," also known as "uncertainty." If the U.S. Treasury proposal recognizes uncertainty for its operational procedures, why do securities policymakers not afford a similar recognition to capital market practitioners? How much longer do they ignore market realities by shoe horning disparate elements in a one-size-fits-all deterministic regime?

Policymakers claim they provide proportionality through exemptible relief. However, when exceptions to the rule become the rule, you need a new rule.

RECOMMENDATION 5: RAISE INTERNATIONAL REGULATORY STANDARDS AND IMPROVE INTERNATIONAL COOPERATION

> *As witnessed in the period beginning in 2007, financial stress can spread easily and quickly across national boundaries. Yet, regulation is still set largely in a national context. Without consistent supervision and regulation, financial institutions will tend to move their activities to jurisdictions with looser standards, creating a race to the bottom and intensifying systemic risk for the entire global financial system.*
>
> *The United States plays a strong leadership role in efforts to coordinate international financial policy through the G-20,[35] the Financial Stability Board, and the Basel Committee on Banking Supervision. The U.S. Treasury will use its leadership position in the international community to promote initiatives compatible with the domestic regulatory reforms described in this report.*
>
> *As outlined in* Financial Regulatory Reform, *the treasury will focus on reaching international consensus on four core issues: regulatory capital standards;*

---

[34] As the adage reminds us, "He who has the gold makes the rules."
[35] Finance ministers and central bank governors from the European Union and 19 nations that represent the world's largest economies.

oversight of global financial markets; supervision of internationally active financial firms; and crisis prevention and management.

At the April 2009 London Summit, the G-20 leaders issued an eight-part declaration outlining a comprehensive plan for financial regulatory reform.

The domestic regulatory reform initiatives outlined in this report are consistent with the international commitments the United States has undertaken as part of the G-20 process. In Financial Regulatory Reform, *the treasury proposes stronger regulatory standards in a number of areas.*

Comment: There is good reason international regulation is "set in largely a national context." In the last quarter of the 20th century, there were approximately 100 stock exchanges formed globally. These exchanges were domiciled in countries that varied dramatically with regard to their economic output and capital market activity. I would like to share some of my five-year experience of frequent travel to the Ukraine to help develop its capital market.

Many emerging markets are balkanized—divided into smaller units that are often hostile toward each other. These markets result from too low standards interacting with too few best-practice operating rules for a given level of commercial activity.

These markets service balkanized industries that are inefficient due to a lack of funding for standardization, which discourages the development of specialized skills. "Stagnant services" emerge when technology lacks the incentive to disintermediate[36] operational redundancies.

Confusion among market participants shortens the time horizon, which further lessens the likelihood of capital investment. This causes variable costs to rise more rapidly relative to fixed costs, with increases in transactional volume.

Ukraine's balkanized industries lacked the scale, scope, speed, and span required by global markets. Enterprises also lacked enabling legislation for specialized services to engage in collaborative commerce.

---

[36] Occurs when investors believe conventional economic methods do not pay sufficient interest to keep pace with inflation and transfer their funds to other economic instruments as a result. This leads to a rapid growth in alternate financial instruments and a loss from traditional institutions, such as savings banks.

At the 2000 PFTS[37] Securities Conference, I was privileged to meet a member of the Ukrainian government's Anti-Monopoly Committee (ACM). During our conversation, the individual told me the ACM had the Ukraine's beer brewing industry under review for potential undue concentration in the commercial market.

Ukraine's three leading brewers, Rogan, Slavutich, and Obolon, generated 1999 revenues of approximately 550,000,000 hryvnas UA (approximately $100 million U.S.). While this may be significant in Ukrainian scale, it is miniscule when compared to the then-Anheuser Busch's $11.7 billion in 1999 global revenues, which comprised approximately 9% of the world market.

The question is which standard—domestic or global—is Ukraine's threshold for a monopoly? Too low a standard for the threshold of a monopolistic commerce creates a lack of critical mass, thereby limiting best-practice operating rules for economies of scale and specialization. Random activity institutionalizes costly labor-intensive business practices. Uncertainty created by nonstandard processing rules causes each market participant to duplicate elements of the transactional process because they are unable to rely upon the efforts of other industry practitioners.[38]

These commercial decisions determine the "national context" that color a country's capital market perspective and argue for segmentation. Similar to education—elementary school, high school, and college—we need to segment depending markets based on their stage of economic development and related randomness of underlying economic conditions.

SCIENTIFIC ANALYSIS OF FINANCIAL REGULATORY REFORM

Let's plug the recommendations from *Financial Regulatory Reform* into Popper's D-N model, outlining the three elements; three operations; and observations.

---

[37] Stock Exchange registered by Ukrainian SEC and in operation since 1997. It's currently the largest market in Ukraine, with more than 150 members and 700-plus securities in the listing. PFTS Stock Exchange is a member of the International Association of Center for Internet Security Exchanges and a correspondent member of the World Federation of Exchanges. PFTS Association owns PFTS Stock Exchange. In October 2006, the Ukrainian SEC extended the period of PFTS self-regulatory organization certificate validity until May 2009.

[38] "GAAMA: A New Perspective for Emerging Markets," Stephen A. Boyko, *International Journal of Economic Development*, Vol. IV, No. 2, April 2002.

The three elements we will use are:
1. The initial conditions are the financial crisis of the Madoff Ponzi scheme and subprime crash of 2008.
2. The final conditions are the policy recommendations listed in *Financial Regulatory Reform*.
3. Scientific laws or universally valid generalizations are the FLITE model's financial standards of fairness, liquidity, integration, transparency, and efficiency.

Our three operations are:
1. Predictions that combine initial conditions with scientific laws,
2. Explanations combine final conditions with scientific laws, and
3. Tests that compare initial conditions to final conditions.

Predictions: Unless regulators segment their one-size-fits-all regulatory regime to evolve risk management into randomness governance (predictability, probability, and uncertainty) and adopt a three-dimensional governance model, they will send confusing and/or conflicting messages (commands that don't correlate to product complexities) to some capital market practitioners. Failure to adapt will also make regulators slow in reacting to the speed with which capital moves.

Initial conditions: The 2008 subprime crash and Madoff Ponzi scheme. The U.S. Treasury acknowledges that its supervisory framework was not equipped to handle a financial dislocation of the magnitude of the subprime crash. To be certain, most of the largest, most interconnected, and most highly leveraged financial firms in the country were subject to some form of supervision and regulation by a federal government agency. But those forms of supervision and regulation proved inadequate.

SCIENTIFIC LAWS: EFFICIENCY
Capital markets are **efficient** if prices reflect all material information. Efficient market hypotheses hold that prices should change only when new information becomes available. Efficiency is a function of the time (speed), effort, and the cost required to change ownership.

A recent move away from the one-size-fits-all mindset was illustrated by the FASB in its amendment of Rule 157, which deals with price discovery establishing fair value. FASB 157 segments the valuation inputs according to whether they are observable, reflecting market activity based on actual transactions from an active market; observable, reflecting comparable market activity; or unobservable, reflecting reporting-entity assumptions from its own data. This hierarchy allows the user of financial statements to assess the relative reliability of fair value measurements more efficiently.

Similarly, Robert Khuzami, SEC Enforcement Division director, confirmed to the *Wall Street Journal* that the SEC is working on a plan to completely reorganize the division by splitting it into teams that specialize in investigating specific kinds of fraud.

"Specialization is a fancy term for being as smart as we can about how we do our job," he said. "By better understanding products, markets, and transactions ... we can better identify trends and patterns."[39]

I am not so sure regulation was unequipped to handle a financial dislocation of the magnitude of the subprime crash. Rather, I believe regulators were slow to react to a changing environment. The growing policy shortcoming is that regulators govern with two-dimensional metrics in a three-dimensional world. Regulators are using maps when they should be using GPS. How efficient can that be?[40]

The consequences may prove even more disasterous, because U.S. regulators face greater demand for resources required by global mass markets and greater complexity required by innovative products.

Explanations: The final conditions in our exercise are the U.S. Treasury proposal's gaps, (over)laps, and naps; scientific laws are integration and efficiency.

Gaps include the treasury's proposal that the "Federal Reserve Board receives prior written approval from the secretary of the treasury for emergency lending under its 'unusual and exigent circumstances' authority."

Observation: In planning for yet unforeseen market contingencies such as "unusual and exigent circumstances," is the U.S. Treasury recognizing "uncertainty"? If the proposal recognizes uncertainty for its operational procedures, why won't securities policymakers afford capital market practitioners a similar

---

[39] Specialization Key to SEC Enforcement Division Overhaul," Bruce Carton, *Securities Docket Global Securities Litigation and Enforcement Report*, May 5, 2009.

[40] "Toxic Regulation: The Threat of Overreaction," Russell Wasendorf, Sr., interviewing Stephen A. Boyko, *SFO Magazine*, July 2009.

recognition? In doing so, this bifurcation in recognition could have the unintended consequence of creating more operational gaps.

Among the overlaps are that Congress, the presidential administration, and financial regulators took significant measures to address some of the most obvious inadequacies in the consumer protection framework, but comprehensive reform was needed. For that reason, the U.S. Treasury proposed the creation of the CFPA, a single regulatory agency, with the authority and accountability to ensure consumer protection regulations are written fairly and enforced vigorously. Consumer protection is a critical foundation for our financial system. It gives the public confidence that financial markets are fair and enables policymakers and regulators to maintain stability in regulation. To this end, the SEC is proposed to protect investors, improve disclosure, raise standards, and increase enforcement.

Observation: If the design was for a single regulatory agency, why are both CFPA and the SEC mentioned? More Washington turf wars? The more moving parts involved, the more likely it is that integration difficulties increase exponentially.

How efficient is duplication of effort? You cannot have shareholder rights that are disproportionate to shareholder responsibilities. Instead of duplicating agencies, wouldn't it be more efficient to have a distance learning center provide consumer finance courses?

The Madoff Ponzi scheme definitely constitutes a regulatory nap. According to news reports, SEC investigators recognized in 2006 that Madoff had misled the agency about how he managed customer money, yet the agency missed an opportunity to uncover an alleged Ponzi scheme.

Documents indicate the SEC had Madoff in its sights amid multiple violations that, if pursued, could have blown open multibillion-dollar scam for which Madoff later received a 150-year prison sentence. Instead, his firm registered as an investment advisor—at the SEC's request—and the public received was kept in the dark about Markopolos's accusations.

Markopolos—who once worked for a Madoff rival—sparked the probe with his nearly decade long campaign to persuade the SEC that Madoff's stated investment returns were too good to be true. The *Wall Street Journal* reviewed emails, letters, and other documents Markopolos had shared with the SEC over the years.

When he first began studying Madoff's investment performance a decade ago, Markopolos told a colleague, "It doesn't make any damn sense," he and the colleague recall. "This has to be a Ponzi scheme."[41]

Observation: With his vision for an organization of specialists, Khuzami appears to be the right man at the right time for the job of enforcement director. While common in U.S. attorney offices, which is Khuzami's background, the model at the Enforcement Division has not been specialization. There, the staff has traditionally worked as a group of specialists who take on the SEC's entire range of cases (i.e., one-size-fits-all). Indeed, given that the Enforcement Division has operated for decades under a generalist model, some describe the move as the SEC's "biggest overhaul since the 1970s" and a "radical departure" from past practices.[42]

Testing: The initial condition is that investors who were overly reliant on credit-rating agencies combined with the final condition. In each case, the final condition was that lack of transparency prevented market participants from understanding the full nature of the risks and uncertainties inherent in the investment.

Observation: Initial condition focused exclusively on risk, while the final condition evolved to discussing risk and uncertainty. Calls for a systemic change within our capital markets should begin with the recognition and attendant disclosure of the prevailing economic environment as either determinate or indeterminate. Thereafter, logic suggests we segment governance regimes to better fit market realities rather than shoe horn diverse economic environments into a deterministic one-size-fits-all legacy governance.

PART III TAKEAWAY: NET BENEFIT IN DOUBT

It will be hard to control the direct cost of duplicative salaries and the indirect cost of integration difficulties resulting from turf wars between governmental agencies. Therefore, a regulatory net benefit that could result from supporting two regulatory agencies is doubtful.

---

[41] "Madoff Misled SEC in '06, Got Off," Gregory Zuckerman and Kara Scannell, *Wall Street Journal*, December 18, 2008.

[42] "Specialization Key to SEC Enforcement Division Overhaul," Bruce Carton, *Securities Docket Global Securities Litigation and Enforcement Report*, May 5, 2009.

The U.S. Treasury's plan to reform regulatory efficacy is problematic. I fear this is a typical bureaucratic ploy for resources—more rules, manpower, and expenses—all to get a bigger hammer to drive a nail more effectively and efficiently.

There were glimmers of hope—appointing Khuzami director of the Enforcement Division, FASB Rule 157, and a segmented approach to threats to financial stability.

But I kept thinking, *Is reshuffling all there is?* Add another letter to the regulatory alphabet soup. Where was SOX, the last financial dislocation's poster child? We get an 88-page proposal, yet not one reference about SOX's future use.

The U.S. Treasury proposal seems to be a structured settlement for stagnant services (Luddite employment for low-tech, high-touch activity) to benefit financial rent seekers.

PART FOUR
Effective Governance

DOING THE RIGHT THINGS

Critical to the success of true financial regulatory reform are the sequence and timing of capital market innovations. To create a societal net benefit requires that these market innovations are both effective and efficient.

This section focuses on effectiveness—doing the right things by segmenting market randomness to better correlate information flows with the introduction of the Entrepreneur Exchange (EntEX), a proportionate regulatory regime tailored to the specific needs of emerging, indeterminate, negative cash-flow growth companies. The next section focuses on efficiency—doing things right by minimizing time, cost, and effort, with the use of three-dimensional governance metrics.

Unlike the alphabet soup typical of regulatory reform, comprehensive governance requires real change. If the U.S. Treasury's reform proposal is to be effective, it needs to go beyond merely reshuffling regulators and throwing more money at the problem. By comparison, I argue for a transformative approach, which will segment governance randomness in terms of predictable, probable, and uncertain regulatory regimes. The latter regime gives rise to a new market structure, EntEX, to serve as the transactional platform for indeterminate issuers.

DISCLOSURE OF RANDOMNESS LIMITS SYSTEMIC FAILURE

How many investors would have bought collateralized debt obligations (CDOs) if there had been full disclosure as to the degree of predictability, probability, and uncertainty of instrument cash flows? Could CDOs have been rated AAA?

CDOs are a type of structured asset-backed security (ABS), with value and payments derived from a portfolio of fixed-income underlying assets. CDOs are assigned different risk classes, or tranches. "Senior" tranches are considered the safest securities. Interest and principal payments are made in order of seniority. Junior tranches offer higher coupon payments or lower prices to compensate for additional default risk.[1]

Billionaire businessman Warren Buffett and others warned that CDOs, ABSs, and derivatives spread valuation risk and uncertainty more widely than they reduced randomness through diversification.[2]

---

[1] *CDO Primer*, Securities Industry and Financial Markets Association.
[2] "What Warren Thinks," Nicholas Varchaver interviewing Warren Buffett, *Fortune*, April 14, 2008.

This is why I argue that calls for systemic change of our capital markets must begin with the recognition and attendant disclosure of the underlying economic environment as either determinate or indeterminate. Thereafter, logic suggests segmenting governance into predictable, probable, and uncertain regimes to better correlate information flows and better fit market realities is better than shoe horning diverse economic environments into one-size-fits-all governance regimes.[3]

The subprime stock market crash of 2008 led to widespread cries to "reign in risk" for effective governance. I contend that what placed our capital market system in jeopardy was not so much risk, but the other component of randomness—uncertainty.

Innovative solutions for global markets resulted in greater complexity. Complexity begat uncertainty, as complex structured financial products evolved from earlier, simpler versions. This required innovative and adaptive changes to address uncertain and unforeseeable circumstances. Over time, the relative percentage per transaction and absolute amount of uncertainty in the capital market triggered a tipping point, leading to chaotic market conditions.

Much like the threat of an avalanche altering mountain pathways in winter, randomness creates strategic change. But does understanding and managing a natural Minsky Moment relate to dynamic, nonlinearities of the marketplace? How do you recognize that point in a credit cycle or business cycle when investors' have cash flow problems due to spiraling debt they have incurred to finance speculative investments? That point where a major market selloff begins, when no counter party can be found to bid at the high level previously quoted? That point that results in a sudden and precipitous collapse in market clearing asset prices and a sharp drop in market liquidity?[4]

In contemporary disaster research, it is generally accepted among environmental geographers that there is no such thing as a natural disaster. In every aspect of a disaster, the causes, vulnerability, preparedness, results and response, and reconstruction contour the occurrence. The difference between who lives and who dies is, to a greater or lesser extent, a social calculus. The term "natural disaster" is an oxymoron.[5]

---

[3] "Best Fit for Best Practice Governance," Stephen A. Boyko, *SFO Magazine*, January 2009.
[4] "In Praise of Hyman Minsky," *The Guardian*, August 22, 2007.
[5] "Introduction to the Sociology of Disasters," Lars Clausen and Wolf Dombrowsky, *Civil Defense Research*, Vol. 14, (Commission for the Protection of the Federal Minister of the Interior, Bonn, Germany, 1983) p. 11-39 and p. 81-102.

There is a subtle but fundamental difference between natural disasters, stock market crashes (processes), and financial crises (events). Jean-Jacques Rousseau first articulated this difference in 1755 when Portugal was shaken by an earthquake. In a letter to Voltaire one year later, Rousseau noted that nature had not built (process) the houses that collapsed and suggested that Lisbon's high population density (process) contributed to the earthquake's toll (event).[6]

In other words, financial crises are exogenous hazards requiring tactical, procedural changes; stock market crashes are the result of endogenous social processes requiring strategic, policy changes.

The vulnerability or resilience of a given system is not simply dependent on the outcome of future events, because vulnerability is the complex product of past political, economic, and social processes, as noted by Rousseau. When hazards such as landslides mix with social systems, the catastrophic nature of disasters may increase.

However, the role of vulnerability as a causal factor in disaster losses tends to be less understood. The idea that disasters can be managed by identifying and managing specific risk factors and uncertainty profiles has only recently become widely recognized.[7] The Department of Homeland Security is an example of a learning curve in progress.

To illustrate the task at hand, let's look at Chaos Theory's sand pile experiment. The system of sand is weakly interactive when you begin building a sand pile. Sand grains drizzled from above onto the center of the sand pile have little effect on the other sand grains. As grains are added to the pile, the pile's slope "self organizes" to a critical state that is at the threshold of instability. At this point the sand pile cannot grow any larger and breakdowns. All different sizes of breakdowns or sand slides are possible. Per Bak[8] refers to this phenomenon as a

---

[6] "Disaster Theory for Techies," Patrick Philippe Meier, *iRevolution*, May 15, 2009.
[7] "Introduction to the Sociology of Disasters," Lars Clausen and Wolf Dombrowsky, *Civil Defense Research*, Vol. 14, (Commission for the Protection of the Federal Minister of the Interior, Bonn, Germany, 1983) p. 11-39 and p. 81-102.
[8] Per Bak (1948-2002) was a Danish theoretical physicist credited for the development of the concept of self-organized criticality.

state of self-organized criticality. The sand grains on the surface of the sand pile have self-organized to a point where they are just barely stable.

What does it mean to say that "breakdowns of all different sizes" can happen at the self-organized criticality state? How does the addition of one more grain result in an avalanche or sand slide?

What are the implications for the management of the capital market? The size of the slide can range from one grain to catastrophic collapses involving large portions of the sand pile. The size distribution of these slides follows a Power law over any specified period. That is, the average frequency of a given size of avalanche is inversely proportional to some power of its size. Big avalanches are rare and small avalanches are frequent. To illustrate, over 24 hours you might observe one avalanche involving 1,000 sand grains, 10 avalanches involving 100 grains, and 100 avalanches involving 10 grains.[9]

Context is reality. Calls for improved compliance must have historical reference to connecting the grains of sand of the governance network. Crises, crashettes, and crashes are constant occurrences in the capital market.

Crises, like the one I had early in my investment career. I had a large position in a gaming stock—the next rocket to riches. The Friday after Thanksgiving it dropped from 14 to 4, due to the loss of a major contract. My entire book—including family members with whom my wife and I to meet at the theater that evening—was invested.

In the midst of this financial version of an Acapulco cliff dive, my branch manager, knowing of my circumstances, came into my office to ask my thoughts. "Alternative career paths," was my response. It was a crisis, but it was my crisis. Other than sympathy and well wishes from my fellow brokers, the stock's plummet affected no one else in the office.

Crashettes, like a 500-point down day—no problem, just Wall Street having a sale, a great buying opportunity. How much buying power do I have?

But, systemic crashes require spotting the "black swan," as Nassim Taleb writes.[10] His book, *The Black Swan: The Impact of the Highly Improbable*, is about

---

[9] Bak, Per. *How Nature Works: The Science of Self-Organized Criticality*, (Springer-Verlag Telos, Emeryville, California, 1999) p. 52.
[10] Taleb, Nassim Nicholas. *The Black Swan: The Impact of the Highly Improbable*, (Random House, New York, N.Y., 2007).

randomness and uncertainty. The term "black swan" comes from the ancient Western belief that all swans are white. Thus, in philosophical discussions the black swan became an oft-cited reference to the improbable. Aristotle's Prior Analytics is most likely the original reference that makes use of example syllogisms involving the predicates "white" and "black" swan.[11]

From a practitioner's perspective, spotting a "black swan" is being able to profile your approach to a self-organized critical event. My frame of reference is that *influencers*—the chair of the Fed, U.S. Treasury officials, investment analysts, etc.,—speak uncharacteristically in undifferentiated clichés, such as saying they will "take a long-term perspective." This indicates that when the critical grain of sand hits the pile and causes a sand slide to begin, decision makers will lack knowledge of the critical variables that control their margin of error. When you cannot control your margin for error, "cheap" and "down" become relative terms.

Deterministic protocols are less than useful in an indeterminate underlying economic environment. Influencers' senses are in a "white-out" condition.[12] Welcome to uncertainty.

This was the case in 1987 that caused me to buy put-protection and/or write calls against large positions. Major mistake. When influencers respond to specific questions with undifferentiated clichés about the virtues of a long-term perspective, look out. Why? Context is reality. They were merely repeating conversations they had had with large institutions. When the 1987 crash commenced, everyone followed the herd. Rampant selling prevailed, with large institutions leading the charge to turn a crisis into a crash.

Similarly with the subprime crash of 2008, evidence from a huge national database containing millions of individual loans strongly suggests that the single most important factor in home foreclosures is negative equity.[13] I posit that cash flow is the bright line differentiating risk and uncertainty in the capital market.

---

[11] Aristotle. *Prior Analytics, Books I and II*, 350 B.C.
[12] A weather condition in which visibility and contrast are severely reduced by snow and diffuse lighting from overcast clouds.
[13] "New Evidence on the Foreclosure Crisis: Zero Money Down, Not Subprime Loans, Led to the Mortgage Meltdown," Stan Liebowitz, *Wall Street Journal*, July 3, 2009. He is professor of economics and director of the Center for the Analysis of Property Rights and Innovation at the University of Texas, Dallas.

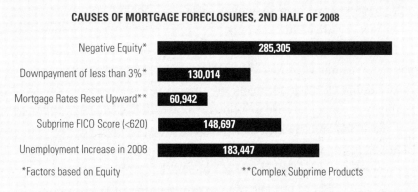

Source: Stan Liebowitz regression analysis of loan-level data in 30 million mortgages compiled by McDash Analytics

Stan Liebowitz, professor of economics at the University of Texas, makes a similar point for the housing market. This is contrary to what many policymakers blame for the rise of home foreclosures. Policymakers argue subprime mortgage lenders presumably misled borrowers to take out complex loans at "teaser" interest rates. Those hapless individuals were then supposedly unable to make the higher monthly payments when their mortgage rates reset upward. But what if, as Liebowitz suggests, the exploited were really the exploiters?

Liebowitz illustrated that the conventional narrative is wrong, using his analysis of loan-level data from McDash Analytics, a component of Lender Processing Services Inc. It is the largest loan-level data source available, covering more than 30 million mortgages.

The McDash data allowed Liebowitz to construct a housing price index at the zip code level and then calculate the current equity position of each homeowner. He was thus able to compare the importance of negative equity to other variables related to foreclosures. In essence, Liebowitz reverse engineered the process to determine that negative equity was the independent variable to control the margin of error.

Understanding the causes of the foreclosure explosion is required if we wish to avoid a replay of recent painful events. Liebowitz concluded that the suggestions offered by the presidential administration and most media outlets—more stringent regulation of subprime lenders—would not have prevented the mortgage meltdown.

While NINJA and LIAR loans gave property rights to renters, Liebowitz demonstrated that the presence of such loans also misdirected policymakers focus on the wrong variables to control the adverse consequences of the crash. As Rousseau noted, crashes usually embody a misguided socioeconomic-political component that further exacerbates the calamity.

Liebowitz demonstrated the need for adaptive, new innovations, and techniques. You cannot effectively govern indeterminate financial instruments (i.e., negative equity mortgages) with one-size-fits-all deterministic metrics. Subprime credit default swaps that tried to insure negative cash flow uncertainty proved to be financial nonsense. From a valuation perspective, complex structured financial products with positive cash flow were marked-to-market, whereas those with negative cash flow tended to be marked-to-model.

The current market turmoil witnessed Minsky Moments of vicious cycles with imploding home price markdowns. If two different elements are joined and treated as the same, difficulties will likely follow. Misstating the independent variable by trying to force a false construct in an effort to reach probabilistic mark-to-market values with uncertain mark-to-model cash flows created a financial avalanche.

RANDOMNESS: GOVERN IT OR IT GOVERNS YOU

One way or another, policymakers are forced to govern randomness. Randomness can be governed proactively by segmenting market randomness in a predictable regime (which is currently in place for money market instruments); a probabilistic regime (which is currently in place for positive cash flow issuers that trade on the NYSE or NASDAQ); and an uncertain regime (EntEX, for negative cash-flow issuers).

Alternatively, policymakers will be forced to govern randomness reactively through exemptive relief. Trying to govern equally a large universe of disparate issuers, investors, and intermediaries with one-size-fits-all regulatory metrics creates unequal results. In an attempt to provide proportionality, regulators have granted relief through exceptions. However, when exceptions to the rule become the rule, a new rule is needed.

Governing randomly creates two unintended consequences from perverse incentives—rule writing and subsidizing market externalities.

As mentioned in Part I, rule writing is the proscriptive description of an undesirable event or process. It does not necessarily produce a net benefit and is not synonymous with governance. Rule writing is ad hoc policymaking that places a bandage over the current problem. It describes the undesirable situation—prefacing it with the admonishment, "don't do this,"—and expects societal buy-in.

SOX is rule writing. And given that it wasn't mentioned in the 2009 regulatory proposal from the U.S. Treasury, it has proven a costly procedural fix of little constructive policy consequence.

The second unintended consequence is that disproportionate governance subsidizes market externalities. An externality, or spillover of an economic transaction, is an impact on a party that is not directly involved in the transaction. In such a case, prices do not reflect the full costs or benefits in production or consumption of a product or service. Externalities (OTC derivative markets) can cause market failure if the price mechanism does not take into account the full social costs and social benefits of production and consumption.[14]

In the article "What is an Externality?" for The Mises Institute, Gene Callahan[15] traces the history of the externality concept back to British economist A.C. Pigou, who developed his theory for both negative and positive externalities.

Pollution is an example of a negative externality. Let's say a factory dumps manufacturing waste into the river. This is a terrible cost to people downriver, because of odor and pollution. Pigou recommended taxing activities that produce negative externalities. Emission taxes on factories are an example of this approach. A positive externality arises when those not directly involved reap some of the benefits from an activity. The traditional policy responses to positive externalities have been for the state to subsidize or require the activities in question. For example, primary education is often said to have positive externalities, such as producing informed citizens.

In the 1930s, British economist Lionel Robbins (1898-1984) challenged Pigou's analysis, noting that economic utility is not measurable. It is invalid to compare levels of utility between different people, as Pigou's analysis required. Robbins recommended using the criterion of Pareto optimality[16] as the basis of welfare economics.[17] A policy has to make at least one person better off and none worse off before economists can say it is unambiguously better. But Robbins held that if we just assume people have an equal capacity for satisfaction, then economists still can recommend certain state interventions.

---

[14] "What is Systemic Risk Today?" Oliver De Bandt and Philipp Hartmann, *Risk Measurement and Systemic Risk (Proceedings of a Joint Central Bank Research Conference, Bank of Japan, 1998)* p. 37-84.

[15] Gene Callahan works in the securities industry and writes frequently for mises.org. He also authored *Economics for Real People: An Introduction to the Austrian School*, The Mises Institute (2001).

[16] Named for Italian sociologist and economist Vilfredo Pareto (1848-1923), it exists when economic resources and output have been allocated in such a way that no one can be made better off without sacrificing the well being of at least one person.

[17] Robbins, Lionel Baron. *Nature & Significance of Economic Science*, Second Edition, (MacMillan and Co., LTD., London, 1945) p. 17-36.

The notion of justifying economic intervention on the basis of welfare analysis was dealt a severe blow in 1956, with the publication of economist Murray Rothbard's essay, "Toward a Reconstruction of Utility and Welfare Economics." Rothbard noted that it is only through preference demonstrated in action that we can gauge what actors really value. Trying to deduce values from mathematical formulas without the evidence of action is a hopeless cause.

When people demonstrate their preferences through exchange, we can say that both parties felt they would be better off trading goods than not.[18] Since Pigou's mark-to-model solution involved imposing taxes and subsidies by fiat (without voluntary exchange), the number arrived at is mere guesswork.

Yet socialistic guesswork is what has been proposed. Why is such guesswork (SOX), superior to *capitalistic* guesswork (highly leveraged securing of negative equity mortgages)?

Now substitute financial pollution—accounting irregularities—for manufacturing pollution and noise traders for the folks living down river, and we can draw comparisons to the tenuous reasoning that led to the disproportionate burden of SOX regulation. The standard of net benefit stands proxy for Pareto efficiency. Demonstrating preferences by exchange and trying to arrive at "guesswork" numbers were problems addressed by FASB 157.

However, trying to protect noise traders with one-size-fits-all metrics creates the unintended consequence of disproportionate regulation for some portion of the market. This will become a negative externality and calls into serious question the U.S. Treasury's proposed regulatory reform to provide a net benefit and achieve Pareto efficiency.

Unintended consequences of such legacy practices include increasing rather than decreasing the volatility attendant to market randomness. Best-practice financial regulatory reform requires separate regulatory regimes that recognize and differentiate determinate from indeterminate economic environments.

Legacy governance practices that fail to distinguish between random underlying economic conditions tend to create results that have proven contrary to intention. The distinction has been well understood for almost 100 years; Frank

---

[18] "What is an Externality?" Gene Callahan, *The Free Market*, Vol. 19, No. 8, August 2001.

H. Knight's 1921 book, *Risk, Uncertainty and Profit*, remains the classic treatment. Knight posited that "risk" referred to those events where decision makers can assign mathematical probabilities to the randomness encountered. In contrast, "uncertainty" referred to events when randomness could not be expressed in terms of mathematical probabilities.

Knight's work was instrumental in reshaping financial industry's risk management and product design practices. His work, however, was largely overlooked by the industry's regulators. Their slowness in adopting industry best practices exacerbated market perturbations during the past 20 years and helped suppress economic development and productivity.

Knight's seminal work provided a plan to decrease uncertainty, which included:
1. Combining uncertainties through larger scale;
2. Increasing control of the situation; slowing throughput; and
3. Increasing knowledge.[19]

What the 2008 subprime crash illustrates is that although established capital market governance is almost exclusively deterministic, the U.S. Treasury's remedies relied heavily on Knight's uncertainty metrics by:
1. Using greater scale to propose a $700 billion Resolution Trust Corporation-type pool for troubled assets;
2. Banning short selling for more than 800 financial institutions from September 19, to October 9, 2008, to exercise greater control over bear raids; and
3. Considering slowing throughput by reinstating the uptick rule.

Surprising by its absence is the call for increased knowledge. Much has been made about the lack of regulatory red flags when complex structured financial products were made available to green mortgagors.

Holding market participants who deal in uncertain investments to the condition of predictability conveys regulatory responsibilities without attendant regulatory disclosures and transparencies regarding whether economic actors operate in a determinate or indeterminate economic environments. If the SEC seeks guid-

---

[19] "The Unanticipated Consequences of Technology," Tim Healy, Markkula Center for Applied Ethics, Santa Clara University, 2008.

ance relative to complex structured financial transactions,[20] then it acknowledges the existence of uncertainty.

This raises a question: Can indeterminate activities be governed by deterministic SOX-type regulation or by deterministic metrics that buttress Paulson's strategies for using Knight's indeterminate best practices to remedy the financial crisis?[21]

Imposing commands to attain predictive capability on capital markets characterized by uncertainty undermines market resiliency and increases the probability of systemic failure. Regulating a market characterized by "uncertainty" as though it were deterministic imposes sanctions on unforeseeable events that stifle free market innovation and adaptability. Government-sponsored regulatory opacity, in turn, creates a moral hazard that places practitioners in jeopardy of being held to a higher deterministic standard than an uncertain economic environment allows.[22]

WHY DO MARKETS SEGMENT AS THEY MATURE?

To properly frame this question requires defining the words "markets" and "segment."

A market[23] is a dynamic, nonlinear system. A market is any structure that allows buyers and sellers to exchange any type of goods, services, and information. A transaction involves the exchange of goods or services for money.

Market participants are all the buyers and sellers of a good, and they all influence its price. This influence is a major function of economics and gives rise to several theories and models concerning the basic market forces of supply and demand. There are two economic actors in markets—buyers and sellers. Whichever has first move advantage determines whether such product is sold or bought. In

---

[20] *Comments on Release No. 34-49695, File No. S7-22-04* (June 9, 2004), from Stephen A. Boyko to Jonathan G. Katz, SEC, regarding a proposed interagency statement concerning complex structured finance activities of financial institutions.
[21] It is interesting to note that the GSEs Fannie Mae and Freddie Mac were exempt from many of the provisions of SOX.
[22] "Random Governance," Stephen A. Boyko, Due Process Institute, 2008.
[23] Sullivan, Arthur and Steven M. Sheffrin. *Economics: Principles in Action,* (Prentice Hall, New Jersey, 2003) p. 28.

capital market vernacular, it is whether the trade ticket is marked "solicited" (sold) or "unsolicited" (bought).

Capital markets underwrite innovative issues that must be sold. These offerings are sold in target markets by refining the transactional processes through "intermediation" and "infomediation."[24] A target market is where the vendor initiates a transaction with a customer. Intermediaries provide sponsorship to compensate for uncertainty, relative to a lack of product information and/or a lack of niche market efficiencies.

Transactions that are bought in reverse markets are self-selected by consumers employing risk management techniques. A reverse market is where the customer initiates a transaction with a vendor. These near-equilibrium transactions are complete with respect to both issuer information and related market efficiencies.

The market facilitates trade and enables the distribution and allocation of resources in a society. Markets allow any tradable item to be evaluated and priced. A market emerges more or less spontaneously (Chaos Theory strange attractors[25]) or is constructed deliberately by human interaction in order to enable the exchange of rights (ownership) of services and goods. Markets are governed by the principles of the FLITE model.

Markets differ from firms in that they are horizontal structures due to their organizational chart being wider than it is higher, whereas firms are hierarchies, with their organizational chart being higher than it is wider. This suggests that markets have more decentralized decision making when compared to the centralized decision making that occurs in firms. Markets and firms treat transparency differently in that markets are open, with disclosure regimes, and firms are closed, with trade secrets protected by patents and non-compete clauses.

Markets and firms also treat transaction costs differently. Firms try to imbed (preserve) transaction costs (i.e., commissions) where as markets try to disintermediate such costs. The "term transaction" cost is frequently believed to have been coined by British economist Ronald Coase. He used it to develop a theoretical framework for predicting when certain economic tasks would be performed by firms and when they would be performed on the market. However, the term is

---

[24] Coined by McKinsey partner John Hagel in his bestseller, *Net Worth*.
[25] The extending and folding of chaotic systems give strange attractors, such as the Lorenz Attractor, the distinguishing characteristic of a nonintegral dimension.

actually absent from his early work up to the 1970s. While he did not coin the specific term, Coase indeed discussed "costs of using the price mechanism" in his 1937 paper "The Nature of the Firm,"[26] where he first discusses the concept of transaction costs.

Arguably, transaction cost reasoning became most widely known through American economist Oliver E. Williamson's *Transaction Cost Economics*. According to Williamson, the determinants of transaction costs are frequency, non-substitutability, uncertainty, bounded rationality, and opportunistic behavior.[27]

Finally, markets differ from firms as to their major expense. The major expense of a market is its infrastructure costs and a firm is its inventory costs. To illustrate, Wal-Mart changed governance structure from being a firm to a market when it created an advanced enterprise software system that allowed it to avoid inventory costs on specific products. Wal-Mart was able to negotiate payment to the manufacturer when the product is scanned at the register. Over time, this type of savings efficiency will enable Wal-Mart to remain a "best of breed" retail marketplace.

Market segmentation at its most basic level refers to subdividing a market along a self-referential or common ground. The purpose of segmentation is the concentration of marketing energy and force on the targeted segment to gain a competitive advantage. In this sense, it is much like the military concept of "divide and conquer."

To segment the market is to divide a larger body into subgroups based upon different needs or product preferences. A key factor in competitive success is to focus on little differences that give a marketing edge and are important to customers. The core concept of market segmentation is AIDA.[28] That is, evolving the customer relation from awareness, to interest, to desire, to action. This process is enhanced by using a technique known as differentiated marketing.

Differentiated marketing builds greater loyalty and repeat purchasing by considering customer needs and wants. Concentrated or target marketing gains

---

[26] Published in *Economica*, p. 386-405.
[27] Reissued by Edward Elgar Publishing in 1995.
[28] Ferrell, O.C. and Micahel Hartline. *Marketing Strategy*, (Thomson South-Western, Florence, Kentucky, 2005).

market position, with specialized market segments. Conversely, an undifferentiated strategy treats the market as a whole, focusing on what is common to the needs of customers rather than on what is different.

Why is this important to a discussion on capital markets? The SEC is marketing protection to investors; that is why. *Financial Regulatory Reform* states, "Consumer protection is a critical foundation for our financial system. It gives the public confidence that financial markets are fair and enables policy makers and regulators to maintain stability in regulation. To this end, the Securities and Exchange Commission is proposed to protect investors."

The SEC uses an undifferentiated regulatory program and one-size-fits-all compliance metrics to market customer protection to a large, differentiated base of retail investors. Given the robust nature of the market, it will not take long for then next round of gaps, (over)laps, and naps to happen and set the stage for the yet another regulatory reform.

The remedy for cross-purpose structural problems that conflict is to develop an effective and efficient governance universe (EEGU).

For the SEC to develop such a universe, the capital market must be segmented into three governance regimes based on randomness:

- One regime for predictable money market instruments with predictable cash flow (i.e., "don't break the buck");
- One regime for probabilistic, earnings-driven, large-cap issues with positive cash flow; and
- One regime for uncertain, event-driven, small-cap issues having negative cash flow.

Such segmentation will enable governance regimes to evidence a high degree of informational correlation.

Market segmentation is a natural byproduct of economic maturation. As markets become more robust, consumers seek financial instruments tailored with increasing precision to meet their needs. For example, when the demand for housing increased in the latter half of the 20th century, the 30-year, fixed-rate mortgage was modified to accommodate different maturities, variable interest rates, negative amortization, and balloon payments. As standardized mortgage niches attained critical mass, they were safeguarded to mobilize capital and drive down the cost of capital.

Questions have arisen as to whether the SEC's one-size-fits-all regulatory approach has reached the point where it creates dislocations that frustrate the processing of information[29] and conflicts with established financial theory.[30]

To illustrate, Nobel Prize winner Harry Markowitz originated basic portfolio theory in the early 1950s. Markowitz was among the first to attempt to quantify risk and demonstrate how stock prices react to financial information.

A correlation coefficient is a measure of the degree to which an issuer's stock price reacts to material market information. The value of the correlation coefficient ranges from -1 to +1. For a value of +1, issuers are positively correlated, and their stock prices move simultaneously in the same direction and magnitude. Issuers that have a correlation coefficient of -1 are negatively correlated, and their stock prices move simultaneously in opposite directions and magnitude. A correlation coefficient of 0 indicates there is no relationship. If a smaller issuer's material information does not correlate with large-cap metrics (and vice versa), each category should be governed under separate regulatory regimes.[31]

MARKET PRACTITIONER PERSPECTIVE

Market practitioners are intermediaries, investors, and issuers.

What is does segmentation do for practitioners? It provides effective governance in a simple, straightforward way to conduct business—the ability to correlate information relative to a system of checks and balances designed to ensure that all are treated fairly in accordance with just and equitable principles of fair trade.

Intermediaries have a great deal of idiosyncratic and complex information with which they must work. (Read: jargon.) To illustrate, *Financial Regulatory Reform* proposed legislative, regulatory, and administrative reforms to promote transparency, simplicity, fairness, accountability, and access in the market for consumer financial products and services.

---

[29] "SEC Extends SOX 404 for Small Public Companies," *Compliance Week*, March 3, 2005.
[30] The insurance industry differentiates in its practices between a "foreseeable" act that is probabilistic in terms of risk management and an "unforeseeable" act that is indeterminate in terms of uncertainty.
[31] SEC comments on Reference: File Number 265-23.

Simplicity you say. Try reading part of the definition for the principle of "liquidity." It is the Net Capital Rule's "undue concentration haircut provision" SEC rule 15c3-1, subparagraph (c)(2)(vi)(M(1). The provision states that in case of:

> "*money market instruments, or securities of a single class or series of an issuer, including any option written, endorsed, or held to purchase or sell securities of such a single class or series of an issuer (other than "exempted securities and redeemable securities of and of an investment company registered pursuant to the investment Company act of 1940), and securities underwritten (in which case the deduction provided for herein shall be applied after 11 business days), which are long or short in the proprietary or other accounts of the broker or dealer, including securities that are collateral to secured demand notes defined in Appendix D, 240.15c3-1d, and that have a market value of more than 10 percent of the "net capital" of the broker or dealer before the application of paragraph (c)(2)(vi) of this section or Appendix A, 240.15c3-1a, there shall be an additional deduction from net worth and/or the Collateral Value for the securities collateralizing a secured demand note defined in Appendix D, equal to 50 percent of the percentage deduction otherwise provided by this paragraph (c)(2)(vi) of this section or appendix A., on that portion of the securities position in excess of 10 percent of the net capital of the broker or dealer before the application of paragraph (c)(2)(vi) of this section and Appendix A. In the case of the securities described in paragraph (c)(2)(vi)(J) the additional deduction required by this paragraph shall be 15 percent."*

Note there are more than 225 words—and that's one sentence. What is even worse is that as a junior research analyst in the NASD's Department of Regulatory Policy and Procedures,[32] I worked on the proposal that brought forth this piece of financial Shakespeare.

Those party to the discussion were knowledgeable regulators. They were smart and experienced, but we spoke our own language. Translating industry jargon into *Reader's Digest* simplicity is a monumental task. The "licensed" have a vested interest in preserving the status quo.

---

[32] Now part of the Financial Industry Regulatory Authority (FINRA).

As an aside: Whenever approached by someone asking if I want to get back into the financial business, I use the undue concentration haircut provision as the starting point for salary negotiations. If you are going to start a broker-dealer, there are three things that you need:
1. Capital,
2. Series 24 License to be a General Securities Principal, and,
3. Series 27 License to be a Financial and Operations Principal.[33]

To be fair, the likelihood of an undue concentration haircut question on the Series 27 examination is somewhat remote, but SEC Rule 15c3-1—the Net Capital Rule—is justifiably an integral portion of the examination. Financial Industry Regulatory Authority (FINRA) is the largest independent regulator for entities doing business in the United States. All told, FINRA oversees nearly 4,900 brokerage firms, about 173,000 branch offices, and approximately 651,000 registered securities representatives.[34] The challenge of governing this complex body is enormous.

But how does this justify market segmentation to better correlate information? Segmentation provides a sharper focus from which to regulate. Rather than a binary "yes/no," "check-the-box" review, specialized staff examiners get to know the relevant portion of the business. This benefits all practitioners.

By extension, segmentation limits the gaps, (over)laps, and naps that were problematic in the 2008 subprime crash. As previously mentioned, *Financial Regulatory Reform* proposes "legislative, regulatory, and administrative reforms to promote transparency, simplicity, fairness, accountability, and access."

"Access," however is a nonprime principle; it is a subset of "fairness." If someone is denying access to a qualified individual, that individual is being treated unfairly. Overlapping principles causes mission creep, which often results in disproportionate governance. It is also symptomatic of rule-based rather than principle-based governance.

Investor segmentation is basic to every financial relationship. Imagine if a news flash occurred regarding a stock in which you, as a broker, had a large

---

[33] Series 28 Financial and Operations Principal license for non-clearing firms.
[34] FINRA.

position. If you did not segment your investor positions, how timely could you respond to investors? What good is best execution if your order is a day late?

The first step in establishing an investor relationship begins with the designation of short-term, intermediate, and long-term financial objectives. These benchmarks should be related to specific a goal, such as funding your child's education to the amount of $200,000 in eight years. The key to managing money is to manage your client's emotions—fear and greed.

Therefore, the next step in segmenting an investor base is to buy investments that your clients know. If the client uses and likes the product, so much the better. This will reduce the degree of fear and greed in the financial equation. Investment portfolios should be diversified, with no fewer than eight issues representing different sectors of the economy. This will reduce most of the diversifiable risk. The portfolio should use as little margin as possible, so as to maintain control of your investment decisions. In addition, 10% of the portfolio should be set aside for special situation investment opportunities. Finally, three months living expenses should be kept in money market instruments as an emergency reserve.

The investment process is further segmented into three lifecycle categories:
1. Less than 40 years of age,
2. Between 40-to-60 years of age, and
3. Older than 60 years age.

For investors younger than 40, a more aggressive randomness profile can be in place. A client needs only to hit one investment homerun to be involved in estate planning rather than tax planning. Between 40 and 60, the investor's portfolio is balanced with the addition of more conservative and income producing securities. When the investor passes 60 years old, if God does not trust in it, the investor does not invest in it. The above comprises approximately 80% of the investment management business; the remaining 20% is split between financial metrics and interesting noise.

So how does market segmentation aid the investor in segmenting his portfolio? By dividing randomness into predictable, probabilistic, and uncertain underlying economic conditions, investors attain greater precision from which to understand their investment priorities, given their age.

Most readers would be surprised as to the precise distinctions investors can make if an investment relates to their personal situation. Market segmentation provides greater context for investor portfolio segmentation. Investors also benefit from a segmented market because it is easier to construct an affinity portfolio driven by knowledge. A knowledge-based approach equates financial capabilities with financial capacity.

I agree with the U.S. Treasury proposal; consumers should verify their ability to understand and use disclosure forms with qualitative and statistical tests. For those who fail to qualify, there should be a distance-learning component to provide a higher understanding of foundational finance.

Issuer segmentation's bright line is a function of cash flow. Issuers with positive cash flow are characterized as determinate, while issuers with negative cash flow are characterized as indeterminate. Until an issuer achieves and maintains a positive cash flow, its existence is dependent upon selling its product/service and selling its corporate stock. This causes the CEO to divide his/her energies between managing the business and selling stock.

Definitions of cash flow are:
- operating cash flow-earnings before taxes plus noncash charges (EBITDA);
- cash flow-net income plus noncash charges; and
- free cash flow-cash flow less contractual commitments and capital budgeting items.

Issuers generating free cash flow are better able to control their environment and don't have to simply respond to their environment. Free cash flow enables issuers to buy back their stock or position their company as a take-over target; merge with or acquire a competitor to reach critical mass; use trade discounts to buy equipment to become a low-cost provider; explore distressed-sale opportunities; issue or increase their dividend; and reduce amount of debt and/or increase debt rating for existing debt, thereby lowering their cost of capital.

Governance should mirror the investment process so rules and information correlate with capital market activity. This requires that the capital market's governance metrics to operate in a manner similar to those by which investors allocate their funds. Accordingly, the capital market should be segmented into three separate regulatory regimes to reflect the fundamental economic conditions by which these markets operate.

There are two generic categories of securities:
- event-driven stocks that are "sold"
- earnings-driven stocks that are "bought."[35]

Of the roughly 15,000 publicly registered companies in the United States, approximately 80% are categorized as micro-cap stocks that are typically "sold." Meanwhile, approximately 20% (i.e., Russell 3000) are categorized as mature stocks that are typically "bought." The capitalization profile of publicly traded securities in the micro-cap market is defined as less than $100 million, the small-cap market range is $100 million to $500 million, and the established market is more than $500 million.

This is somewhat higher than the small business standard that is defined in Rule 405 of the Securities Act of 1933. Generally, a small business that has $25 million in sales or capitalized market value qualifies as a small business issuer. It is estimated that there are at least 3,000 OTC Bulletin Board and Pink Sheet-quoted[36] companies, which have capitalization in excess of $25 million.

Within every economic trend, there exists a reflexive volume-value dynamic.[37] At the outset, compatible and/or complementary components of the trend are grouped to achieve critical mass. Thereafter, segmentation takes place, as successful niche components attain materiality to evolve from a Sarnoff to Metcalfe network.[38]

We now appear to be at the aggregation-segmentation function's inflection point, given the increased societal importance of SMEs. This provides economic strategists and academicians with an opportunity to revisit these concepts and refine their thinking, relative to the issues involved and their level of accuracy

---

[35] For a detailed discussion of bought vs. sold, reference SEC comment letter on "Qualified Purchaser," File S7-23-01, which can be downloaded at http://www.sec.gov/rules/proposed/s72301/saboyko1.htm.

[36] Companies quoted on the Pink Sheets do not need to meet minimum requirements or file with the SEC; also refers to OTC trading.

[37] In the early years of NASDAQ it advertised the daily volume of its issuers, whereas the NYSE advertised the capitalization of its issuers.

[38] This is often referred to as an AIDA (awareness, interests, decision, and affinity) conversion. Today, AIDA conversions happen to a greater degree at a greater frequency. Remember: Radio took 38 years to reach a critical mass of 50 million users; TV, 12; and e-commerce, four.

and precision in understanding descriptive terms used for effective and efficient economic policy.

Economists hold that for every seller there is a buyer, and vice versa. Whether you agree or disagree, the key issue from a financial market perspective is who initiated the transaction—the buyer or seller.

Classical economics supporting "bought" regulation is a product of the 17th century's Age of Enlightenment and is devoted to the study of equilibrium. The concept of equilibrium works well in a bounded rationality of the U.S. Treasury market, but the precision of the process is questionable when stress-tested under chaotic conditions of the micro-cap market's "sold" construct. Equilibrium is the product of an axiomatic system that is in a constant process of adjustment (near-equilibrium versus far-from-equilibrium conditions). It starts by taking supply and demand curves as a given to produce a unique market clearing price. The idea that supply and demand may be independent or interdependent of one another—or dependent on market prices—was not considered in the 17th century.[39]

The regulatory dilemma confronting the SEC is, given different pricing and sales-practice metrics for event-driven stocks that are "sold" as compared to earnings-driven stocks that are "bought," can both be governed effectively and efficiently with the same regulatory regime?

ENTREPRENEUR EXCHANGE

SMEs around the world face a common problem: obtain a "sliver of equity" to enable their operations to achieve growth and positive cash flow.

This is alarming, as SMEs are crucial to economic growth, given their potential for job creation, innovation, commercial aggregation, and integration of global capital markets. I posit that the core difficulty SMEs face in their pursuit of equity financing is not investor indisposition to SMEs, but a fundamental failure of the SEC's one-size-fits-all approach to regulating equity securities.

---

[39] Soros, George. *Open Society,* (Perseus, New York, N.Y., 2000) p. 50-53.

As a result, I propose the formation of a micro-cap market designated as the EntEX, with a governance approach that is specifically tailored for indeterminate SMEs.[40]

SMEs and micro-cap markets are easy to ignore when establishing regulatory policy, given their relatively small size and limited analyst and media coverage. But micro-cap SMEs drive the efficient use of resources and facilitate trade between parties with different comparative advantages that accelerate the generation, dissemination, and application of innovative ideas.

It is troubling that while the bull market at the end of the 20th century witnessed the globalization of capital markets, almost all of the benefit flowed to firms that traded on top-tier U.S. markets, such as NYSE and NASDAQ. SMEs were unsuccessful in obtaining financing.

To this end, David Weild and Edward Kim of Grant Thorton LLP wrote an article titled "Why are IPOs in the ICU?"[41] Their research indicated that in the last several years the IPO market in the United States has practically disappeared.

That's because the market for underwritten IPOs, given its current structure, is closed to most (80%) of the companies that need it. Further, their research shows that the pre-dot-com bubble period for the IPO market underwrote about the same number of IPOs as the dot-com bubble timeframe. Yet, the pre-dot-com bubble period had more than three times more IPOs than the post-dot-com bubble period.

On average, there were 520 IPOs per year leading up to the dot-com bubble. The number of IPOs post-bubble has fallen nearly 30%, to 134 IPOs per year. Also troublesome is that the median age of a venture-backed company at the time of the IPO reached 8.6 years in 2007, with the longest "gestation period" on record dating back to 1991.

Why have SMEs faced so much difficulty obtaining equity financing? There are two generic categories of equity securities: event-driven stocks that are "sold"

---

[40] This section is comprised of excerpts from articles I wrote about the EntEX: "Small is Beautiful," with Aron Gottesman, Ph.D., *The National Interest*, No. 77, Fall 2004; "How the SEC Impedes the Growth of Small Business," *Yorktown Patriot*, May 26, 2006; "Small and Micro Caps Suffering From SEC's Uniform Regulations," *Seeking Alpha*, May 30, 2006; "Capital and the Small Businessman: A Proposal for an International Entrepreneurial Exchange," *In The National Interest*, May 21, 2003; and "Entrepreneurial Exchange," *Research Magazine*, October 2003.

[41] "Why are IPOs in the ICU?" David Weild and Edward Kim, Grant Thorton LLP.

and earnings-driven stocks that are "bought." Top-tier, large-cap stocks tend to be earnings-driven and are categorized as bought. They are priced as a multiple of their cash flow, earnings and/or dividend. The risk associated with these top-tier stocks is measurable, using earnings information from financial statements. This measurability implies that a probabilistic, expected-value assessment can be determined using modern portfolio risk management techniques.

Conversely, micro-cap stocks are "sold" and event-driven. Examples of an event may be a new contract or product announcement. The valuation of micro-cap stocks is a function of either their corporate mission, percentage of market share, or price-to-sales ratio relative to their evolutionary stage of development. Further, the lack of a history of earnings means that investors face uncertainty, which is distinct from risk insofar as it cannot be measured, and is therefore difficult to manage.

Until micro-cap equities realize their critical corporate event that enables them to generate positive cash flow, they remain in a state of self-organized criticality. Management focuses on playing defense by minimizing its burn rate.

Because micro-cap issuers need to finance cash flow shortages, the supply of issues to be "sold" is their independent variable. But if these issues are primarily sold, how can this be reconciled with Rule 502(c) of Regulation D [Rule 502(c)], which prohibits issuers from general solicitation and general advertising in private placements?

Given those limitations, many issuers find it difficult to attract investors. Imagine going to a supermarket that would let you walk the aisles without letting you know what products were on sale.

The current regulatory regime is incompatible with and inappropriate for micro-cap investors, and inefficient and ineffective for SME capital formation. The exigencies of EntEX governance can be demonstrated best by the contrapositive (proof in the negative) of the current one-size-fits-all regulatory regime's lack of micro-cap success. Previous regulatory experiments such as the SCOR 504 Program, the ACE Net Project, and the IPO Net Project were compromised with "bought-lite" regimes imposed on the SME "sold" construct. None achieved the hoped-for success.

The existing one-size-fits-all SEC regulatory regime places a disproportionate focus on financial capacity relative to financial capability that is biased toward top-tier, earnings-driven stocks that are bought.

The SEC contends its policies are appropriate to manage the regulatory divide between sold and bought securities. The commission believes its considerable regulatory experience with the use of the term "accredited investor" strikes the appropriate balance between the necessity for investor protection and meaningful relief for small business offerings.

Yet like much of SEC governance, the accredited investor test is primarily a measure of financial capacity to self-insure that neither addresses an investor's financial sophistication nor differentiates financial knowledge relative to securities that are sold from securities that are bought.

So what's the solution? Given the difficulties associated with regulating sold micro-caps using regulation tailored to bought securities, EntEX seems a viable answer.

EntEX will be a separate Internet-based micro-cap trading system with delivery-vs.-payment settlement and clearance. EntEX's fundamental characteristic will be a unique regulatory regime that shifts the emphasis away from investor financial capacity (net worth and income) to investor financial capability (specific micro-cap knowledge and investor sophistication).

Under EntEX's patented governance, a micro-cap association would maintain a registry of investors who satisfactorily completed their coursework and/or who are "grandfathered in," pursuant to demonstrated prior expertise. This registry would serve, absent fraud, as a safe harbor to the provisions of the 1933 Securities Act and 1934 Securities Exchange Act.

Investors who do not meet the above-criteria could still transact micro-cap issues subject to the current regulatory regime. Similarly, the association would qualify and maintain a registry for all financial intermediaries not subject to prior statutory disqualification. Registered corporate advisers would, among other things, help obtain financing, facilitate secondary market activity, and disseminate corporate information of micro-cap issuers. These intermediaries would have minimal regulatory requirements and would include not only existing registrants but also attorneys and accountants, who act as finders.

The key benefit of EntEX is that it reduces the cost of being a public company by substituting investor intellectual capital for financial capital. EntEX's registry of certified investors employ core competencies based upon their specific knowledge, relative to the CEO's capability; the specific innovative product/process; general industry expertise; and/or SME capital formation metrics to attain a comparative advantage for reducing micro-cap investment uncertainty. EntEX's governance creates a niche market for sophisticated investors, where compliance costs are priced more efficiently at the margin for only those services actually needed.

Although against prevailing regulatory trends, a securities regime that emphasizes regulating investors would enable a low-cost, market-driven approach to governance. No mandatory regulations are necessary for investors with good information on micro-cap market issuers.

A core principle of EntEX's transactional process is that investors should be financially sophisticated and therefore not need regulatory "protection" when offered or sold securities of micro-cap issuers. EntEX would create a preferred shoppers network for participants in the micro-cap market through consumer education and market infrastructure enhancements. In turn, lower regulatory-related costs and liability considerations would encourage the conduct of business onshore.

Another benefit is that EntEX provides a forum for greater transparency, which enables investors and issuers to select an appropriate form of micro-cap sponsorship. EntEX's scalable sponsorship enables foreign emerging and U.S. micro-cap issuers to form strategic alliances in a network that generates an exponential wealth effect. Issuers have an obligation to be factually accurate with what they disclose. How much they choose to disclose is determined by issuer discretion. Information asymmetries then become the first analytical screen.

Micro-cap informational profiles are an additive supply chain process. Each increment of information is a value-added input that contributes an additional unit of wealth for each item provided. An issuer interested in corporate governance and transparency relative to prospective corporate finance has incentives to put forth an appropriate level of disclosure that is scalable to the perceived benefit. Interested issuer agents and certified investors reciprocate by providing incremental, scalable sponsorship. As the micro-cap issuer's critical event approaches, investors and intermediaries will scale investment analytics from sold to bought.

Market reforms are a function of regulatory and infrastructure enhancements. To this purpose, EntEX metrics recognize the difference between event-driven stocks that are "sold" in the micro-cap market and earnings-driven stocks that are "bought" in the top-tier market. It provides proportionate regulation that is compatible and appropriate for a registry of sophisticated micro-cap investors. EntEX infrastructure facilitates effective and efficient capital formation for SMEs. Its vision of a "sold construct" enables the "sliver of equity" to be underwritten for SME organic growth and reduces the regulatory divide between global capital markets for SME strategic growth.

The potential for dynamic increase in the percentage of wealth created by EntEX's governance process and financial infrastructure is similar to the economic transformation that occurred when the United States changed the foundation of its government from the Articles of Confederation to the Constitution.

ENTEX APPLICATION

EntEX can be used for public as well as private sector functions. Consider the reluctance of some states to accept stimulus money. Most of these states have to confront the unenviable spread of high unemployment and a low revenue base. Such is the case of my home state of South Carolina.

South Carolina Governor Mark Sanford argued he could not put the funds to use profitably. Trading today's cash flow problem for tomorrow's financial crisis is a Hobson's choice—a free choice in which only one option is offered, colloquially formulated as "take it or leave it." Unless our policymakers can demonstrate a profitable use for such funds, it also is a choice where stakeholder rights are excessive to stakeholder responsibilities.

South Carolina's economic problem is that our legislators talk of *cuts* to the exclusion of productive economic *growth*. This path inevitably leads to class warfare. Moreover, the ultimate in economic "cutting" is to liquidate the state. Replace "South of the Border" signs with "South Carolina going out of business—all reasonable offers considered."

There are three forms of economic growth: portfolio (organic growth of existing enterprises); foreign direct investment (attracting enterprises from outside the state and captured retirement money); and entrepreneurial ventures (creation of new products or markets).

Unfortunately, lack of a robust economic vision has rendered South Carolina as an extract economy; unless you can grow it (agriculture), enjoy it (tourism), and/or provide low-cost alternative labor to make it, South Carolina lacks the capability to participate in high multiple, value-added revenues. The outward migration of our talented college graduates illustrates the problem.

South Carolinians need garden parties to grow commercially viable enterprises more than they need TEA ("taxed enough already") parties. EntEX would provide a platform where stimulus funds could be applied to create wealth and employment.

THE CONTRAPOSITIVE ARGUMENT:
EINSTEIN'S SEARCH FOR UNIFICATION

This will make some scientists wince. But for illustrative explanation—not scientific rigor—consider Albert Einstein's failure in pursuit of scientific unification to suggest that the capital markets need to segment.

For this purpose, I will use the contrapositive technique. The contrapositive is a proposition derived by negating and permuting the terms of another equivalent proposition. This is done because sometimes it is easier to prove a result in the contrapositiveform than in the original conditional form. Proving the contrapositivemight also be done as a direct proof, by induction or by contradiction. Whether it is better to prove a statement in the original form or to rewrite it to an equivalent form is difficult to answer.[42]

But let's examine Einstein's last scientific challenge—unification—for guidance in financial regulatory reform and the need for market segmentation.

There are four fundamental forces within all atoms. They dictate interactions between individual particles, and the large-scale behavior of all matter throughout the universe. They are the strong and weak nuclear forces, the electromagnetic force, and gravitation.[43]

These forces are to science as the FLITE model principles are capital market governance. Because it appears that all known interactions between objects can be described with only four fundamental forces, Einstein asked, "If only four, then

---

[42] www.math.csusb.edu/notes/proofs/pfnot/node7.html.

[43] A strong nuclear force binds the protons and neutrons that comprise an atomic nucleus, preventing the mutual repulsion between positively charged protons from causing them to fly apart. This interaction is the source of the vast quantities of energy that are liberated by the nuclear reactions that power stars. The weak nuclear force causes the radioactive decay of certain atomic nuclei. In particular, this force governs beta decay, whereby a neutron breaks up spontaneously into a proton, electron, and antineutrino. The weak force is responsible for synthesizing different chemical elements in stars and in supernova explosions, through processes involving the capture and decay of neutrons. The electromagnetic force determines how electrically charged particles interact and magnetic fields. Like charges repel each other; unlike charges attract. The electromagnetic force binds negatively charged electrons into their orbital shells around the positively charged nucleus of an atom. This force holds atoms together. Gravitation is a force of attraction that acts between every particle in the universe. It is always attractive—never repulsive. It pulls together matter; gives objects weight; keeps a moon in its orbit; and binds galaxies in clusters.

why not only one?" Perhaps all interactions between matter can be described in terms of one master force. This is what the SEC is trying to do for administrative simplicity—to the chagrin of market reality.

The quest for unification of forces is indeed an intriguing one. It captured Einstein's imagination. He pondered it for the last 30 years of his life—a fruitless search for a unified field theory. But for Einstein and his few unification-minded colleagues, the big issue was to unify general relativity—a theory of gravity—with Maxwell's electrodynamics.

It is difficult to accuse Einstein of leaving stones unturned, no matter how unpromising they might appear. It seems that the real significance of Einstein's quest for unification lies in its quixotic ambition.[44] Simply stated, if Einstein was unable to produce a one-size-fits-all approach for science, why does the SEC persist in using a one-size-fits-all approach for the capital market?

PART IV TAKEAWAYS

Warren Buffett and former IMF chief economist Raghuram Rajan warned that CDOs, ABSs, and derivatives spread valuation risk and uncertainty more widely than they reduced randomness through diversification. Absent segmentation of randomness, a societal net benefit from *Financial Regulatory Reform* seems unlikely.

When "influencers" respond to specific questions with undifferentiated clichés about the virtues of a long-term perspective, look out. They are repeating their conversations with large institutions. When the 1987 crash commenced, everyone followed the herd. Rampant selling prevailed, with large institutions leading the charge to turn a crisis into a crash.

Understanding the causes of the foreclosure explosion is required if we wish to avoid a replay of the 2008 subprime crash. Suggestions for more stringent regulation of subprime lenders would not have prevented the mortgage meltdown. While NINJA and LIAR loans gave property rights to renters, Liebowitz demonstrates that the presence of such loans also misdirected policymakers focus on the wrong variables to control the adverse consequences of the crash.

The presence of an active shadow market in an economy indicates the extent to which existing economic policies are either inappropriate or inefficient for a

---

[44] "Einstein's Quest for Unification," John Ellis, *Physics World*, January 5, 2005.

given level of commerce. The shadow market serves as a low-multiple surrogate for the standard capital market and constrains wealth creation. It subsidizes economic rent seekers and free riders, offshore intermediaries, and underground finders—at the expense of domestic issuers and investors.

The SEC uses an undifferentiated regulatory program and one-size-fits-all compliance metrics to market customer protection to a large, differentiated base of retail investors. Given the robust nature of the market, it will not take long for then next round of gaps, laps, and naps to happen, setting the stage for the yet another regulatory reform.

Creating jobs in the absence of wealth is a false construct. EntEX enables and enhances both labor and capital components of production.

PART FIVE

Efficient Governance

STREAMLINE THE MARKET THROUGH SEGMENTATION

Efficiency is the process for reflexively managing the dynamic governance forces of societal stability and societal change, as illustrated in the **Reflexive Management of Dynamic Governance Forces** matrix on page 127.

These forces are subdivided into categories of structures (i.e., economic actors and platforms) and processes (i.e., regulation) to form an efficient governance universe (EGU). An EGU occurs when material information evidences a high degree of correlation with regulatory protocols for transparency and commercial activity.

MARKET EGU

To develop an EGU, the capital market needs to be segmented into three components: one for predictable money market instruments; one for probabilistic, earnings-driven, large-cap issuers having positive cash flow; and one for uncertain, event-driven, small-cap issuers having negative cash flow.

With regard to the formation of the latter, an innovative capital formation and trading structure called the EntEX was proposed in Part IV. The three-dimensional GAAMA model's feedback system monitors Pareto[1] financial transactional efficiency. The growing policy shortcoming stems from regulators governing with two-dimensional metrics in a three-dimensional world. Regulators are using maps when they should be using GPS.

Capital market governance is a reflexive process involving commands and incentives.[2] As illustrated in the **Normative Governance Model** on page 128, regulators create governance regimes by choosing appropriate commands for the incentives available in the economy. Commands and incentives are different sides of a governance equation for a given level of economic activity. They are self-referential; one cannot be discussed in the absence of the other.

Command costs attendant to shareholder rights, enforcement activities, and efforts to limit rent-seeking schemes correspond with incentives derived from

---

[1] Barr, Nicholas A. *The Economics of the Welfare State*, Second Edition (Stanford University Press, Palo Alto, California, 1993) p. 105. Pareto efficiency describes any improvement that can be made without making any other individual poorer. Named for Vilfredo Pareto, who used it in his studies of economic efficiency and income distribution.
[2] "Fit Regulation to Market Reality," *SFO Magazine*, April 2009, Stephen A. Boyko.

Reflexive Management of Dynamic Governance Forces

DYNAMIC GOVERNANCE	STABILITY	CHANGE
Process	Market EGU Predictable Probable Uncertain	Self-organized criticality Rent seeking Free riding
Structure	Corporate Large-cap Small business Industrial Policy Regimes Government Agencies	Intrapreneur Entrepreneur GAAMA Market Externalities Controlled Offshore Balkanized Underground

To create an EGU, material information must align with regulatory protocols. This results in transparency and commercial activity.

shareholder responsibilities and opportunities for free riding. Normative market efficiencies evolve from this process.

The command side of the governance equation is comprised of shareholder rights, enforcement activities, and rent-seeking components. Shareholder rights are a composite of principles and rules.

Principles are prospective societal policies that define industry effectiveness in terms of "the right things to do." They are represented by the FLITE model. Principles are defined in terms of mass, indicating the number of people affected by the command, and materiality, indicating the relative importance of the command.

On the other hand, rules are the retrospective codification of best-practice procedures that define operational efficiency in terms of "doing things right." They are industry proscriptions that explicitly delineate organizational limits in terms of gravitas and granularity. Incentives are the expectation of reward, which induce action or motivate effort in seeking a net benefit, measured in terms of economic profit. The incentive side of the governance equation is comprised of shareholder responsibilities and free-riding components.

Shareholder responsibilities are the attributes of a good financial shopper—primarily a function of pricing and practice metrics, which ensure investors are not overcharged and/or misled.

Normative Governance Model

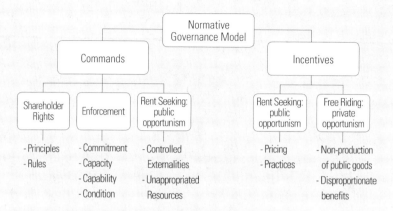

The command side includes rights, enforcement, and the possibility of rent seeking. Incentives come from the enticement to generate economic profit and free-riding opportunities.

Creating efficient capital market governance in a 24-hour-a-day, seven-day-a-week global environment is a formidable task. It starts with an understanding that capital markets are dynamic, nonlinear systems. Consideration must be given to each defining component of a capital market:

- Dynamic—an interactive process characterized by continuous change from competing or conflicting forces
- Nonlinear—one or more chaotic equations whose effects are not proportional to their causes
- Systems—integrated networks consisting of input, throughput, output, and feedback processes

Efficiency is a measure of the transactional cost, time, and effort to change ownership.

Costs must be analyzed relative to their potential benefit. Expenditures that do not provide a societal net benefit are subsidies. Such subventions are inefficient and work as a disincentive to adaptive innovations, as opined by two former SEC commissioners.

According to the former commissioners, "Regulatory action aimed at eliminating every vestige of fraud in a given market would place such a heavy and costly burden of compliance upon issuers that investors would be safe but unable to achieve any meaningful return on their investments. The regulatory agency would also incur a high cost of enforcement. Carried to its logical end, investor protection as a sole reason for regulation—without also granting markets the freedom to reward those who take risk—ironically keeps investors safe and yet fails to fully protect the investors' sole interest in investing in the first instance: to achieve the highest return commensurate with their individual tolerance for risk."[3]

Thus, regulatory proposals designed for top-tier market, risk-management regimes tend to be disproportionate when applied to the micro-cap market. Not so much from the capital expended but from the lack of commercial relevancy to the potential societal net benefit.

When considering time, remember that the duration required for transactional throughput is directly proportional to the level of systemic financial sophistication. A regulatory model focused on investor capabilities has the adaptability to change as these developments occur. This adaptability contrasts with the conventional focus on financial data, which requires change to be retrospective in regulation—typically a reactive and time-consuming process.

Effort represents the number of interested parties required to complete a transaction. Creating a "preferred shoppers" network for small-issuer investors would reduce the number of noise traders who lack specific small-issuer analytical metrics. This would increase the level of compliance through knowledge-driven consumerism.

Small-issuer markets are characterized by poor liquidity and imperfect competition. Given these characteristics, any system that reduces the proportion of unsophisticated investors also will have the benefit of limiting the diversions from fundamental value caused by such noise traders.

Limiting the investor universe to those classified as sophisticated greatly diminishes the noise trader effect, resulting in more effective and efficient governance.

Regulators create governance regimes by choosing appropriate commands for the set of incentives available in the economy. This balances command costs attendant to shareholder rights, with incentive benefits derived from shareholder responsibilities. Otherwise, promulgating rights in excess of responsibilities reduces to unlegislated subsidies, which often spawn economic bubbles. Bubbles are antithetical to market efficiency.

MODELING SELF-ORGANIZED CRITICALITY

From a societal perspective, structures and processes attain Pareto efficiency through reflexive dynamic tension. Through the intrusion of rent seeking and

---

[3] Dissent of Commissioners Cynthia A. Glassman and Paul S. Atkins, "Proposed Registration under the Advisers Act of Hedge Fund Advisers" SEC proposed rule, File Number S7-30-04.

free riding, agents of change are misdirected to create bubbles of self-organized criticality—those that are self-sustaining.

Commentators have noticed that unsustainable bubbles in asset prices have become the mainstay of U.S. policymaking. Market bubbles are price distortions and emanate from two basic sources:

- A tsunami of paper currency that leads to excess liquidity, overflowing hard assets and resulting from bad fiscal and/or monetary policy; or
- The financial equivalent of pate de foie gras—a force-fed system resulting from bad regulatory policy, which immobilizes the flow of capital.

The proverb, "fool me once, shame on you; fool me twice, shame on me," is sage advice for capital market reform. "Change" must be managed efficiently. If not, free-riding and rent-seeking interests will continue to self-organize to a critical level of instability to fool the marketplace. Similar to Chaos Theory's sand pile experiment, there will be a growing number of dollars landing on the capital pile to create Minsky Moments. This will lead to more frequent stock market crashes—in increasingly larger amounts.

We have defined rent seekers as economic actors who manipulate the economic and/or legal environment. In general, the term is associated with government regulation and misuse of governmental authority. Rent seekers claim to protect investors, but in reality, they extract uncompensated value from unappropriated resources without making a commensurate contribution.

As noted in Part III, Congress contemplates clawbacks for financial executives and directors who allegedly shirked their fiduciary responsibility. If that is the case, the same standard be applied to regulators and members of Congress, given their oversight of the GSEs—Fannie Mae and Freddie Mac.

An August 2008 article in *The Washington Post*[4] noted that after the extended period of "loose mortgage lending" was poised to devastate the nation's housing market, Federal National Mortgage Corporation (Fannie Mae) chief executive Daniel H. Mudd wrote a confidential memo to his board.

---

[4] "Fannie's Perilous Pursuit of Subprime Loans: As It Tried to Increase Its Business, Company Gave Risks Short Shrift, Documents Show," David Hilzenrath, *The Washington Post*, August 19, 2008.

According to *The Post*, Mudd's mentions Fannie Mae's successes, noting that one of the company's 2006 achievements was to expand involvement in the subprime market and other nontraditional mortgage products (calling it a "step toward optimizing our business").

It's helpful to point out that these actions align with the preconditions for GAAMA:

- Misapplying tactics by using retrospective rules to plan;
- Mischaracterizing the initial condition, resulting in a disproportionate level of commands to incentives; and
- Misspecifying commercial activity to equate risk with uncertainty.

According to *The Post* article, Fannie Mae outlined plans a month earlier to further expand its subprime-market ventures. In addition, the company recognized the already weak performance of subprime loans but predicted they would get better in 2007, according to another Fannie Mae document.

The Post article also revealed internal company documents showing that even late in the housing bubble, Fannie Mae was drawn to risky loans by a variety of temptations, including the desire to increase its market share and fulfill government quotas for the support of low-income borrowers.

Since then, Fannie Mae's exposure to loosely underwritten mortgages has resulted in billions of dollars in losses and sent its stock price plummeting.[5] This prompted the federal government to prepare for a potential taxpayer bailout of the company. As of July 2009, Fannie Mae reported that loans issued from 2006 and 2007 accounted for almost 60% of its second-quarter credit losses.

Fannie Mae documents obtained by *The Washington Post* from that period paint a picture of two corporate perspectives: fostering affordable housing and making money; and increasing market share while avoiding excessive risk.

In the end, juggling these demands, led Fannie Mae executives to take risks they "either misunderstood or unduly minimized."[6]

Where was the Congressional oversight of the rent-seeking regulators? How beneficial was SOX in controlling these potential problems?

---

[5] "Fannie's Perilous Pursuit of Subprime Loans: As It Tried to Increase Its Business, Company Gave Risks Short Shrift, Documents Show," David Hilzenrath, *The Washington Post*, August 19, 2008.
[6] Ibid.

Compensating for this regulatory resource shortage requires investors to become qualified. Without a proportionate increase in investor financial knowledge, regulation merely dumbs-down the consumer base—at the expense of market efficiency. This creates a moral hazard where unsophisticated investors receive a regulatory subsidy to expand the scale, scope, and span of their investment activity.

Qualifying investor suitability enables the SEC to become more efficient by substituting intellectual capital for financial capital.

Free riders are the private sector equivalent of rent seekers; they consume more than their fair share of a resource or shoulder less than a fair share of the costs. They create economic slippage through governance errors of omission.

The resolution lies in finding a way to prevent free riding from taking place. Consider the role of finders—those who act as unregistered broker-dealers. A broker-dealer is any individual or firm in the business of buying and selling securities for itself and others. Broker-dealers must register with the SEC.

Yet attorneys and accountants have successfully argued that when they act in the role of finders, they assist private companies in obtaining start-up capital. They argue that finders should be a new, federally registered subcategory of broker-dealers, whose activities would be exempt from federal and state broker-dealer regulations. That is the definition of free riding.

STRUCTURES OF STABILITY

The **Macroeconomic Governance Matrix** illustrates the structures by which the forces of stability organize their normative commercial activity.[7]

Note that this matrix combines conceptual constructs that analyze ranges of economic activity, relative to transparency and profitability. The binary byproducts of these constructs are markets, firms, government agencies, and industrial policy regimes, such as GSEs.

All four of these alternative modes of governing economic activity can function complementarily and provide the economy with complex coherence and commercial differentiation.

---

[7] "The Governance of Outsourcing," Stephen A. Boyko, *In the National Interest*, March 17, 2004.

Macroeconomic Governance Matrix

TRANSPARENCY / PROFITABILITY	OPEN	CLOSED
Commercially Viable	Market	Firm
Self-sustainable	Government Agencies	Industrial Policy Regimes

The above illustrates how forces of stability organize their standards and structures for commercial activity. As a result, this matrix analyzes ranges of economic activity relative to transparency and profitability. Resulting byproducts of this process are markets, firms, government agencies, and industrial policy regimes.

The transparency construct addresses the treatment of information. Accurate and timely information increases valuation multiples and market liquidity. Strategic transparency decisions in financial markets are determined to a large extent by the dominant investor.[8]

In general, bank-controlled, debt-driven firms prefer less information attendant to stock market trading. This tends to protect firms in a weak competitive position. Conversely, equity shareholders prefer more disclosure to promote the strategic advantage of firms in a strong competitive position (i.e., higher price-earnings ratio).

The United States is predisposed to investment banking and equity-driven markets, whereas foreign markets are predisposed to commercial banking and debt-driven markets.

The prime determinant for profitability is the political preference for either maximizing profits in the commercially viable private sector or maximizing participation in the self-sustainable public sector.

Commercially viable enterprises tend to employ a marginal-cost model (profits are maximized, where marginal revenues equal the marginal cost of the nth product sold).

Self-sustainable entities are inclined to use an average-cost model. For example, the U.S. Postal Service delivers a letter for the same rate, irrespective of

---

[8] "Dominant Investors and Strategic Transparency," Enrico Perotti and Ernst-Ludwig von Thadden, *Journal of Law, Economics, and Organization*, 2005, Vol. 21, No. 1. Under imperfect product market competition, the corporate transparency decision affects the value of equity and debt claims differently.

whether the letter is to be delivered across the street or across the country. This demonstrates an industrial policy enterprise.

These constructs, with their binary benchmarks, combine to design a robust model for governance.

Markets are dynamic, nonlinear systems. They enable commercial activity to occur at arms-length, using individual liability metrics. To assess and mitigate individual risks, market societies require a significant investment in rules and infrastructure to make price information available. A market's "openness" leads to the development of disclosure regimes for information requirements.

Industrial policy regimes are self-sustainable entities that maximize participation through the use of an average-cost model. Fortunately, the U.S. system of government, with its strong state and local authorities, decentralized economy, and powerful interest groups, has demonstrated its immunity to central planning.

Created by the U.S. Congress, GSEs like Fannie Mae are financial services groups and well-established in the nation's commerce. Their function is to enhance the flow of credit to targeted sectors of the economy and make those segments of the capital market more efficient and transparent. Free market advocates regard such an economic intervention by industrial policy regimes as socialistic.

Government agencies, such as the SEC, have a mission to "protect investors and maintain fair, orderly, and efficient markets." Such agencies serve the social welfare by policing the capital market. To that end, the mission's standard should be to provide a societal net benefit.

Firms or hierarchies govern through a command and control structure. This has a highly developed capacity for centralized strategic planning. Firms tend to be closed in nature and can be subdivided to the microeconomic structures of stability and structures of change, as illustrated in the **Microeconomic Governance Matrix for Structures of Stability** on page 135. This matrix consists of ownership and opportunity conceptual constructs that interact to create binary byproducts of corporate firms, small businesses, intrapreneurs, and entrepreneurs.

Now let's analyze the matrix in detail.[9]

---

[9] "Exploring Entrepreneurship: Lessons Not Found in Business School," Stephen A. Boyko, *Pace University Business Journal*, Nov.15, 2004.

Microeconomic Governance Matrix for Structures of Stability

OWNERSHIP / OPPORTUNITY	DIVERSE (take a job)	CLOSELY HELD (make a job)
Stability with conventional products that are bought	(Model A) Corporate firms: mass market	(Model B) Small business: comfort and conventionality

Opportunity differs from enterprises that seek change from those that wish to preserve stability. Firms that seek stability are corporations and small businesses that market conventional products. There are two fundamental types of products in an economy: innovative products (i.e., a new salsa) that are "sold" to a target market;[10] and, conventional products (i.e., pasta) that are "bought" in a reverse market.[11]

Manufacturer representatives provide product information and transactional infrastructure to initiate transactions of innovative goods and services that are "sold" in target markets.

Conversely, consumers self-select the conventional, "bought" products, such as pasta. The sold-bought product demarcation is determined by whether transaction costs are allocated to the sales department (commissions) for products that are "sold" in target markets or to the marketing department (salaries) for products that are "bought" in reverse markets.

Small businesses, as illustrated in Model B of the matrix, are owned independently and provide conventional products that are "bought." SME owners aggressively market to create affinity relationships, providing superior service in geographic locations where they have a comparative advantage.

Small businessmen and women tend to work to their comfort level, as defined by their community standards. Their desire to preserve capital is greater than their desire to gain additional wealth. This, in part, results from their cash flow dependency and related focus on exit scenarios, access to credit, and tax minimization strategies.

---

[10] A market for new products is where a customer is identified specifically with a Social Security or telephone number.
[11] A market for existing products is where a customer is profiled with a ZIP or area code.

Microeconomic Governance Matrix for Structures of Change

OWNERSHIP / OPPORTUNITY	DIVERSE (take a job)	CLOSELY HELD (make a job)
Change with innovative products that are "sold"	(Model C) Intrapreneurs: corporate innovators	(Model D) Entrepreneurs: innovators for change

This matrix contrasts intrapreneurs and entrepreneurs and demonstrates their interdependence.

STRUCTURES OF CHANGE

The hierarchies that see opportunity in terms of change, with innovative products that have to be "sold" are intrapreneurs and entrepreneurs.

An intrapreneur is someone who displays entrepreneurial qualities as an employee within the framework of the established corporation.

In **Microeconomic Governance Matrix for Structures of Change**, Model C is the product of diverse ownership and someone who sees opportunity in the form of change. Intrapreneurs are likely to be new product/business development oriented. They often fulfill the function of quality control for new products produced by entrepreneurs. The intrapreneur's main task is to determine whether an innovative product can be distributed through conventional channels of a large enterprise. They are problem solvers in decentralized corporations that encourage individual initiative.

Intrapreneurship also is an alternative to outsourcing. This governance profile can be described as follows:

1. Management policies and procedures derived from best practices;
2. Decision structures based on clearly delegated lines of responsibility;
3. Personal autonomy limited and controlled through standards, results, budgets, and reporting chain of command;
4. Conforming environment; and
5. Critical mass considerations.

Entrepreneurs are pragmatic problem solvers. Joseph Schumpeter, the patron saint of entrepreneurs, opens his book, *Capitalism, Socialism, and Democracy*, with a refutation of Karl Marx.

Schumpeter concludes that capitalism's demise will not come about in the way Marx predicted but by "creative destruction."[12] Schumpeter used the phrase to describe a process in which the old ways are endogenously destroyed and replaced by new ways. He looked to the entrepreneur to solve a contemporary problem with a new product, a new process, and/or a new market.

Entrepreneurs are unique people. Much like Benjamin "Bugsy" Siegel's vision of Las Vegas in the Nevada desert, entrepreneurs solve societal problems we didn't know we had. In a competitive environment, entrepreneurs provide goods and services that consumers have always wanted but never quite knew how to produce and/or acquire.[13]

Understanding the nature of entrepreneurs—especially successful entrepreneurs—is not simply an intellectual exercise. For SME investors, the ability to distinguish between a skilled entrepreneur, merchant, and a charlatan is crucial. SMEs are little more than a collection of ideas. The ability to convert these ideas into future profit streams is dependent on the entrepreneurial skills of the founders, whose human capital represents the most valuable asset of the enterprise.

The defining feature of the closely held ownership benchmark is that owners sign a check, thereby investing their own money to "make a job." These owners also see change as an opportunity.

The profile of an entrepreneur is:
1. Independent—do not like someone having authority over them;
2. Craves achievements—most believe they can do the job better than anyone else can. They tackle problems immediately and are persistent in their pursuit of their objectives;
3. Self-confident when they are in control of what they are doing. They will strive for maximum responsibility and accountability;
4. Opportunistic—see different realities and strive to exert their influence; and
5. Cash-flow dependent—they like to hear the ice crackling under their feet.

---

[12] Schumpeter, Joseph Alois. *Capitalism, Socialism, and Democracy*, (Harper Perennial Modern Classics, New York, N.Y., 2008) p. 81-86. Process of transformation that accompanies radical innovation by entrepreneurs, thereby creating sustained economic growth and competition for established companies.

[13] "Understanding Entrepreneurs," Stephen A. Boyko, *In the National Interest*, March 31, 2004.

Entrepreneurial Governance Matrix

ORIENTATION / PERSPECTIVE	CONVICTION (Define Themselves)	CONSENSUS (Defined by others)
Abstract	Dreamers	Dealers
Concrete	Doers	Doubters

"Dreamers" and "dealers" are conceptual, while "doers" and "doubters" tend to focus on concrete tasks.

Entrepreneurs can be categorized through an orientation construct that defines leaders in terms of "conviction" or "consensus" and a perspective construct that defines their view of the world in either abstract or concrete terms.

This produces four categories of profiles: dreamers, dealers, doers, and doubters (the **Entrepreneurial Governance Matrix**).

Dreamers are visionary leaders of conviction who live in the conceptual world of abstraction and specialize in seeing the big picture of broad societal trends. Dealers view the world in terms of abstraction by building consensus. Doubters are numbers-oriented leaders of consensus who respond to concrete opportunities.[14]

THREE-DIMENSIONAL ANALYSIS: THE GAAMA MODEL

The GAAMA model[15] is a three-dimensional depiction of the interaction of normative and non-normative controlled, offshore, balkanized, and underground market externalities.

This dynamic tension creates change. The normative market involves conventional, "bought" products. Here the customer makes the first move (i.e., going to the supermarket for groceries or buying books on the Internet).

---

[14] "Reality is Contextual: Politics and Economics in the Newly Independent States of the Former Soviet Union," Stephen A. Boyko, *In the National Interest*, April 14, 2004.

[15] Modified from the model I presented in 1997 at the Ukrainian Capital Market Conference and subsequent articles and a SEC comment letter I wrote (SEC comment letter on Release No. 34-49695, File No. S7-22-04, June 9, 2004).

Top View of the GAAMA Model

This top view of the GAAMA Model shows the interaction of normative and non-normative markets—externalities classified as controlled, offshore, balkanized, and underground.

The non-normative market consists of externalities, or GAAMA markets, which are comprised of innovative or unique products that require the aid of a specialized salesperson to transact. Externalities also may arise, due to the need for lower transactional cost.

The GAAMA model is a capital market feedback system that provides three-dimensional governance in the relationship between commands and incentives. Graphically, the model represents profit potential attendant to the internalization of transaction costs and conversion of "dead capital" (repatriation).

The GAAMA model illustrates a three-dimensional conceptual shift. It is a nonlinear, dynamic paradigm. GAAMA is an acronym for:
- Global: widespread, having both mass and materiality
- Asynchronous: not timely information
- Asymmetrical: unequal access to information
- Market: dynamic, nonlinear financial system
- Activity: researching, pricing, transacting, clearing, settling, and inventorying

The GAAMA model also functions as an economic knowledge transfer system that combines rules and standards to analyze non-normative ranges of economic activity. Like Alice's "looking glass," the model demarcates the normative from the non-normative externalities by an informational correlation divide. It provides metrics and understanding to normalize non-normative commercial activity.

Governance Evolution

CRITERIA / AGE	DIMENSIONS	DESCRIPTORS	ILLUSTRATIONS
AGRICULTURAL	1-dimensional	Linear, unidirectional	Dominoes
INDUSTRIAL	1-dimensional	Linear, binary	Checkers
DIMENSIONS	2-dimensional	Dynamic nonlinear	Chess
DIMENSIONS	2-dimensional	Cross functional	Rubik's Cube

This chart provides a historical context that reflects the factual realities for revolutionary events and how such events have influenced current decision-making.

The model aids capital market practitioners and policymakers, who often make serious mistakes by basing decisions on disconnected reality; they believe "what has always been so" and what they "wish were so." The foundation for effective and efficient regulatory decision-making is a careful understanding of the facts, which leads to remedial action that minimizes time, cost, and effort.

As noted in the **Governance Evolution**[16] matrix, the Agricultural Age that occurred during the 18th and 19th centuries saw a massive and rapid increase in farming productivity. The agricultural model is represented by a linear vector—a locus of points with the same slope moving in a single direction through space. Governance was an additive, unidirectional function dependent upon familial lineage. Production was a linear, unidirectional function of tillable acreage.

Scale was the primary driver of the Industrial Age. People went from making goods in their own homes with simple tools to making them in large factories with complicated machinery. The goal was to produce things people would buy. Division of labor required specific skills. Jobs represented income opportunities that enabled laborers to move up a vertical organizational chart.

The Information Age was characterized by the ability of individuals to transfer information freely through instant access to knowledge. Such access was previously impossible or difficult. The digital economy transmitted information via a

[16] "Regulatory Rubik's Cube," Stephen A. Boyko, *SFO Magazine*, June 2009.

two-dimensional, (length and width) nonlinear net. People learned by observing and analyzing.

A major differentiator between the aforementioned epochs was that assets employed in the creation of value depreciated with usage in the Industrial Age, whereas they appreciated from usage in the Information Age.

Three-dimensional models drive economies of span and speed to broaden enterprise parameters in the Conceptual Age. However, capital market policymakers too often chose overly simplified responses. These responses were formulated within the context of a relatively narrow, two-dimensional perspective, resulting in unintended consequences (i.e., SOX).

Policymakers must either segment the current one-size-fits-all governance paradigm into predictable, probabilistic, and uncertain regimes in a single three-dimensional governance model or apply two-dimensional matrices and schematics in a coordinated three-dimensional metric. The pathways are different, but the results are the same. A three-dimensional conceptual change must take place for the U.S. capital market to remain competitive in a global economy.

The GAAMA model is a diagnostic tool for measuring the degree of societal compliance with the established governance. Its vertical y-axis represents qualitative standards—those that denote quality. The horizontal x-axis represents quantitative rules, illustrating quantity. The perpendicular z-axis represents the relationship between incentives and commands available to the economy. Together, this three-dimensional model provides proportionate Goldilocks governance; everything is just right—or as right as it can be in a random environment.

The y-axis accounts for the qualitative function of the FLITE model's principles. To that end, it holds that too high standards are exclusionary operational price supports that direct order flow, while too low standards are indiscriminate price controls that act as a disincentive to commercial activity.

As illustrated by the operational support line of **Qualitative Shortage vs. Qualitative Surplus**, (dotted line, Ps1: Qs1), governance supports create exclusionary regulations, which result from too high standards that limit competition and drive the order flow line to an oligopolistic, controlled market (dark gray-shaded area). It also can drive order flow to an offshore market (light gray-shaded area) to meet unfulfilled demand.

The profit premium, as measured by the solid line (Ps: Qs), is the excess cost of inefficient policy borne by the consumers. Policies that limit market activity result in capital rationing and/or economic stagnation. Capital commands order

Qualitative Shortage vs.Qualitative Surplus

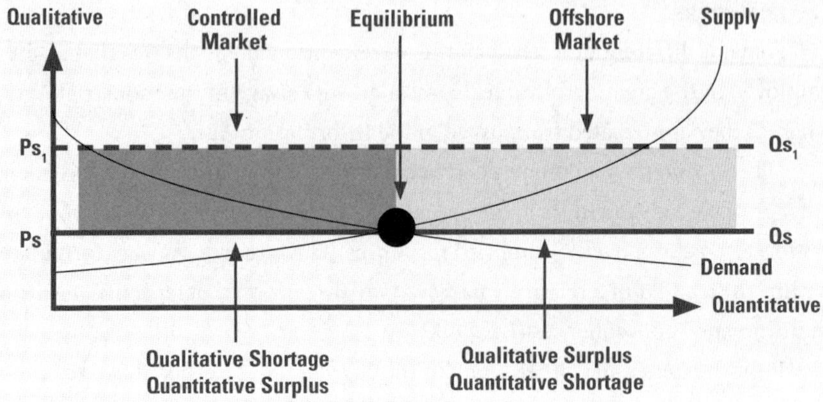

The dotted line (Ps1: Qs1) shows how governance supports create exclusionary regulations. These limit competition and drive the order flow line (dark gray) to controlled market. It also can drive the order flow line to an offshore market (light orange). The solid line illustrates the profit premium (Ps: Qs). It is the excess cost of inefficient policy, which is passed to consumers.

flow, as anti-consumer, high standards foster unresponsive oligopolies that provide incentives to foreign competition.[17]

In **Underground Vs. Balkanized Market** on page 143, the y-axis is defined in terms of mass, or the number of people affected, and materiality, indicating the relative importance. Too-low principle standards are indiscriminate price controls that limit the scale of normative commercial activity. The price control line (Pc1: Qc1) shows how excessive government price controls resulting from too-low standards limit the incentive to produce. As the chart demonstrates, such controls can either push the market underground (dark gray) to cure the quantitative supply/service shortages line and/or a balkanized market (light gray) to cure the qualitative supply/service shortages line.

Too low standards create pricing inefficiencies, which require a high-risk premium in underground markets. In balkanized markets, nonstandard products incur high transaction fees from excessive due-diligence costs.

[17] "GAAMA: A New Perspective for Emerging Markets," Stephen A. Boyko, *International Journal of Economic Development*, April 2002, Vol. IV, No. 2.

Underground vs. Balkanized Market

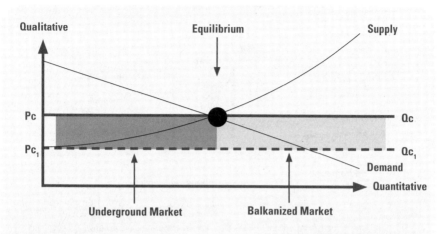

The y-axis represents the qualitative function—"mass," showing the number of people affected,) and "materiality," indicating the relative importance. The x-axis depicts the quantitative function of rules. The price control line (Pc1: Qc1) demonstrates how excessive government price controls result in an underground market (dark gray) and/or a balkanized market (light gray).

The x-axis in **Underground Vs. Balkanized Market** depicts the quantitative function of rules. Rules are the retrospective, codified best practices that support standards (i.e., the Net Capital Rule supports the principle of liquidity).

Too many rules or best practices result in fact confusion and/or conflict (i.e., U.S. tax code). Conversely, too few rules or best practices lead to ambiguity, due to a lack of information or detail (new computer program without the help desk).

The GAAMA model delineates commercial activity resulting from too many/too few rules to resolves bad trade practices.

The **Side View of the GAAMA Model** on page 144 shows the z-axis, which represents the incentives-to-commands ratio. Incentives are the expected reward that induces action or motivates effort in seeking a net benefit, measured in terms of economic profit.

Normative market activity provides a greater wealth effect compared to market externalities, because its return is a function of sales, cash flow, or earnings multiple. Conversely, market externalities are a combination of present value and the cost of compliance avoidance.

To envision the workings of the z-axis the side view, imagine an umbrella: The higher the ring on the umbrella shaft holding the ribs, the greater the normative coverage from externalities.

Side View of the GAAMA Model

This side view of the GAAMA Model shows the z-axis, representing the incentives-to-commands ratio for a given level of commerce. Logic dictates that the higher the ratio, the larger the normative market activity and greater the ability to provide a societal net benefit in terms of economic profit.

The changes in the level of economic activity are a series of small, normally distributed Gaussian changes.[18] What varies is not the amount of commerce conducted but where it is conducted. Once economic activity attains a critical level of commerce, regulation does not stop but merely specifies where the activity is likely to be conducted and how much it will cost to conduct it. Economic activity either going beyond or falling short of the normative operating range then creates externalities of controlled, offshore, balkanized, and underground markets.

The informational divide is the boundary that separates the normative market from non-normative market externalities. Normative markets are a continuous function. This means that there is no sudden change in their value. Notwithstanding bureaucratic attempts to gerrymander a one-size-fits-all regulatory regime, market realities determine compliance boundaries by their informational domain. This requires that a regulatory regime's domain of material information correspond and correlate to governance commands in a continuous function that preserve the domain's limits.

---

[18] Denoted by a bell curve at the mean, it describes the distribution of information that gathers around an average point.

Informational discontinuities resulting from principle standards that are either insufficient or superfluous create market externalities that are governed by separate metrics. The value proposition of the GAAMA model builds upon proven market and mathematical metrics to uncover the principles of global governance. This goes beyond simply profiling patterns of governance that differentiate normative markets from market externalities.[19]

NON-NORMATIVE STRUCTURAL CHANGES: GAAMA MARKET EXTERNALITIES (FRACTALS)

GAAMA markets are fractals: self-similar economic patterns that repeat themselves in far-from-equilibrium, controlled, offshore, balkanized, and underground market externalities.

GAAMA markets are self-similar governance structures that function the same regardless of scale. Fractals can be used to manage randomness in an indeterminate underlying economic environment as the atmosphere adjusts for the shortcomings of Brownian motion.[20]

Regularity in irregularity is important, as each time cycle will have the same fractal pattern. A fractal dimension is the measurement of the imperfect world in which we live.

Reality has been simplified to a tutorial state to deal with complexity. Self-similarity (i.e., a snowflake is a triangle that repeats itself,) is the organizing principle of fractals. Fractals will maintain their same dimension regardless of the scale used.

Controlled markets result from too-high standards interacting with too many operating rules for a given level of commercial activity. Controlled industries need to be deregulated to balance product requirements with market realities. "Sunset" provisions should be incorporated into existing operating rules to reduce redundancies and confusion. This either can occur formally, through operational restructurings and/or financial reorganizations, or informally, by rightsizing the scale of GAAMA operations relative to the level of commercial activity.[21]

---

[19] "Think Before You Regulate: Choose a Better Model," Stephen A. Boyko, *SFO Magazine*, May 2009.
[20] Ibid.

The subprime meltdown illustrated controlled markets with financial institutions that were deemed "too big to fail." Many important financial firms were referred to as too big to fail, such as American International Group, Citibank, and Merrill Lynch.

This results in an inefficient capital market policy that encourages moral hazards.

Moral hazards rely on the government as the lender-of-last-resort. Government bailout loans are priced on the average cost-of-capital to maximize participation for those most in need (as compared to the marginal cost-of-capital to maximize profits, e.g., Citibank will pay a higher rate than J.P. Morgan).

Ending the idea that large financial institutions are "too big to fail" is a top priority under the Obama administration's regulatory reform proposal, said Sheila Bair, chair of the Federal Deposit Insurance Corp.

In a June 2009 interview, Bair told CNBC, "Clearly, there has been moral hazard and lack of market discipline fed by the 'too big to fail' doctrine. … (T)his, in turn, has been fed by the lack of resolution mechanism that really works for very large financial organizations, and this has been a central focus of ours."[22]

Yet it was regulation that gave many of the aforementioned financial institutions the motivation to merge. Regulators sanctioned these mergers.

Regulation does not create competition; it fosters large, unresponsive oligopolies. Oligopolistic business drivers focus on the economies of scale to absorb the overhead costs of regulation and become a controlled market externality.

In a June 2009 *Wall Street Journal* opinion piece, Jamie Dimon cautioned that "ensuring the ability to innovate is also fundamental to U.S. competitiveness. The financial industry is global and highly mobile. If innovation is stifled in America, then capital will simply flow to other nations where it is welcome. That would translate to the loss of jobs, tax revenue, and growth at a time when we can least afford it."[23]

---

[21] "GAAMA: A New Perspective for Emerging Markets," Stephen A. Boyko, *International Journal of Economic Development*, April 2002, Vol. IV, No. 2.
[22] "'Too Big to Fail' Doctrine Must End: FDIC's Bair," JeeYeon Park, CNBC, June 19, 2009.
[23] "A Unified Bank Regulator Is a Good Start," Jamie Dimon, *Wall Street Journal*, June 27, 2009.

In June 2009, *The Economist* opined:

Financial regulation in America has two problems: There is both too much of it and too little. Multiple federal agencies oversee the financial system: five for banks alone, and one each for securities, derivatives, and the government-sponsored mortgage agencies. They share these duties with at least 50 state banking regulators and other state and federal consumer-protection agencies. Yet all these regulators failed to anticipate and prevent the worst financial crisis since the Depression, because risk-taking flourished in the cracks between them. Toxic subprime mortgages were peddled by lenders—with little federal oversight—and shoved into off-balance-sheet vehicles. The greatest leverage accumulated in firms that avoided the capital requirements of banks.[24]

We know the problem but seem unable to distance ourselves from the habit of buying yesterday's reform because policymakers, like the Wizard of Oz, dislike surprises more than they dislike repeating history.

Offshore markets result from standards that are "too high" interacting with "too few" best-practice operating rules for a given level of economic activity.

The lack of savings from too few best practices does not equal the cost of higher standards. The result? A combination of exclusionary pricing and operational ambiguity causes domestic issuers to seek foreign markets as the low-cost alternative.

This occurs because the cost of domestic compliance is greater than the benefits derived from the Law of Comparative Advantage: Every tax and/or regulation imposed on the normative market that is excessive, relative to the level of commercial activity, serves as an offshore subsidy.[25]

The economic factors of production are land, labor, and capital. Outsourcing is the transfer of all or a portion of production's labor component to an external location.[26] The three types of outsourcing are sovereign, surrogate, and structural.

---

[24] "Reforming Financial Regulations in America: Better Broth, Still Too Many Cooks," *The Economist*, June 18, 2009.

[25] "GAAMA: A New Perspective for Emerging Markets," Stephen A. Boyko, *International Journal of Economic Development*, April 2002, Vol. IV, No. 2.

[26] Foreign Direct Investment (FDI) is the transfer of the capital component of production to an external location. Colonization is the transfer of the land component of production to an external location.

Sovereign outsourcing occurs when production is transferred to another country. Those who rail against outsourcing should consider that a significant number of American jobs rely on foreign firms "outsourcing" jobs to the United States. Surrogate outsourcing occurs when production is transferred among political subdivisions within the same country (i.e., plants moving from one state to another). Structural outsourcing occurs when innovation causes existing production to become obsolete, resulting from a shift in skill sets.

To begin improving comparative advantages and core competencies, we must redesign products and retrain people. The old corporate culture must be replaced. Otherwise the iron law of oligarchy will centralize power, ossify operational components, and stagnate the thought processes in an attempt to retain control. Financial institutions are currently experiencing structural change in the wake of the 2008 subprime meltdown.[27]

The London Stock Exchange's AIM includes a wide range of businesses—from early stage, venture capital-backed companies to the more established—because they seek access to growth capital.

Because of its diverse network of professionals and investors, AIM is the most successful growth market in the world. As noted in Part II, AIM powers the companies of tomorrow and continues to help smaller and growing companies raise the capital needed for expansion.

AIM's rise coincided with SOX, which perhaps contributed to AIM success in becoming the market of choice for growth companies worldwide. AIM has benefited from tax breaks offered to investors, as well as its reduced regulatory requirements. This makes it cheaper and easier for companies to make an IPO, pull off future acquisitions, and comply with day-to-day regulatory and investor requirements. As a result the cost of capital on AIM can be cheaper.

Startups around the world used to head to the NASDAQ when they wanted to go public. But since the passage of SOX, IPOs are moving offshore.

Even U.S. companies list themselves on foreign stock exchanges. To this end, the SEC's Advisory Committee on Smaller Public Companies fretted over the SOX effect on IPOs. It was well known that the committee kept an eye on IPO activity

---

[27] "The Governance of Outsourcing," Stephen A. Boyko, *In the National Interest*, March 17, 2004.

abroad. During the meeting, members asked whether the U.S. regulatory regime had frightened away small companies and had contributed to capital formation abroad or whether IPO activity on foreign stock exchanges merely indicates a globalization of the capital markets.

There also are many IPOs being done on AIM that just wouldn't be possible in the United States. AIM is what NASDAQ used to be—a global junior market for emerging companies.

NASDAQ, for example, is no longer suited to companies with market capitalizations under $250 million, while the ideal capitalization on AIM is between $50 million to $500 million. At this level, there is a liquidity advantage for AIM.

Similarly, The Australian Small Scale Offerings Board (ASSOB) seems ready to take its place along side the AIM. First conceived more than 20 years ago, ASSOB formed to operate as a platform to assist SMEs originate, aggregate, and trade unlisted securities.

ASSOB is now one of the largest introducers of private investment to early-stage, high-growth companies, through its network of accredited members. It works within and relies upon the regulatory environment imposed by the Australian Securities and Investments Commission and the Corporations Act of 2001. ASSOB uses many of the techniques used by stock exchange-listed companies, enabling unlisted companies to access up to $5 million in private capital.

It is unique to Australia and fast becoming known as one of the most innovative private capital-raising systems in the world. ASSOB recently launched its Secondary Board, which is the first of its kind in the unlisted securities sector in Australia.[28]

If U.S. financial services become more of a controlled market, will SMEs develop of pathway to AIM?

Unfortunately the lack of a robust economic vision may render the United States an extract economy. Unless you can grow it (agriculture), enjoy it (tourism), and/or provide low-cost alternative labor to make it, America may lose the ability to participate in high multiple, value-added revenues.

Balkanized markets result from standards that are too low interacting with too few best-practice operating rules for a given level of commercial activity.

[28] Source: ASSOB.

Balkanized industries are inefficient because they lack standardization, which discourages the development of specialized skills.

Stagnant services emerge when technology lacks the incentive to disintermediate operational redundancies. Confusion among market participants shortens the time horizon, which further lessens the likelihood of capital investment. This causes variable costs to rise more rapidly, relative to fixed costs with increases in volume.[29]

Part IV discussed EntEX in detail, introducing a new regulatory approach logical governance parallels to AIM. EntEX would require advisors and investors to demonstrate that they have SME specific knowledge and sufficient sophistication. This knowledge would in turn allow them to analyze and value young entrepreneurial firms that have a history of cash flows characterized by constant transformation. A regulatory model focused on advisor and investor capabilities can adapt to change as these developments occur. Knowledge ensures a solid foundation from which to build a robust capital market.

Underground markets result from a combination of enforcement standards that are too low and have too many operating rules for a given level of commercial activity. The nexus of the indiscriminate pricing of societal compliance and operational confusion creates an environment where the benefits from shadow activity (illicit and illegal pursuits, i.e., drugs, prostitution, and tax avoidance) are greater than the penalties for non-compliance. Confusion among market participants shortens the transactional time horizon that necessitates a liquidity premium to consummate transactions. Underground markets have difficulty evolving beyond self-sustenance.[30]

As previously noted, attorneys and accountants are often confronted with the issue of whether and under what circumstances transaction-based compensation can be paid to an intermediary—a finder, business broker, or investment banker—who is not registered as a broker-dealer.

No law or rule clearly sets out the parameters of permissible conduct for a finder, so we must turn to SEC No-Action letters for guidance. There have been

---

[29] "GAAMA: A New Perspective for Emerging Markets," Stephen A. Boyko, *International Journal of Economic Development*, April 2002, Vol. IV, No. 2.
[30] Ibid.

very few No-Action letters regarding intermediaries in mergers and acquisitions. Many of the SEC letters consist only of general statements of law and refrain from No-Action positions.[31]

Here is the dilemma: Entrepreneurs, SMEs, and other microeconomic agents of change need to be able to raise capital. It is becoming increasingly difficult to raise proportionate slivers of equity under the current governance system. We need to find a way to accommodate finders that is acceptable to the regulators. But as a result of a combination of a tighter enforcement language that was broadly interpreted in the past [Section 3(a)(4)(A) of the Securities Act Exchange Act of 1934] as well as a push for greater transparency, we may extinguish a segment of the U.S. business community that is truly needed for the post-subprime recovery.

As attorney Joseph W. Bartlett notes:

There is a long history to this issue, going back to the early days of securities regulation, when the authoritative guide was Professor Loss's treatise on the Securities Regulation. Loss took the view that 'finders,' meaning agents who were paid to assist in private placements and who did not engage in any of the other usual business activities of a broker-dealer (retail sales; custody of customer capital; underwriting; etc.), were not required to register under Section 3(a)(4)(A).

Relying (either consciously or unconsciously) on Loss's point of view, literally thousands of organizations have sprung up in this country—firms which perform functions as finders and help arrange placements, typically in consideration of a success fee. Several years ago, however, the staff announced, in a series of No-Action letters, that it did not believe there was a so-called 'finders exception' to Section 3(a)(4)(A). (T)he staff has stuck to that point of view ever since, despite a good deal of public criticism that the position went too far. The objection was, and is, that pure finders, who do not engage in any of the other traditional activities of brokers/investment bankers, should be exempt, or at least treated differently. Were they all required to register, they would be undergoing unnecessary administrative and legal expense in complying with a complex set of rules and guidelines."[32]

---

[31] "Current Challenges to Smaller Companies under Disclosure and Corporate Governance: Capital Formation and Making 'Finders' Viable," Hugh H. Makens, Warner Norcross &, Judd LLP, SEC Government-Business Forum on Small Business Capital Formation, September 20, 2004.

[32] "Unregistered Finders: Can Issuer's Counsel Participate in the Deal?" attorney Joseph W. Bartlett, VCExperts.com.

The answer is "broker-dealer lite" in an EntEX governance regime. This would enable finders to register in accordance with the current position of the SEC staff without becoming unduly burdened with administrative regulatory issues.

FUTURE WORLD: THE REGULATORY RUBIK'S CUBE[33]

Rubik's® Cube

Financial regulatory reform of the legacy governance system requires a three-dimensional evolution.

The proposed Regulatory Rubik's Cube builds upon proven market and mathematical decision metrics to uncover governance principles rather than simply profiling governance patterns. It holds that regulation in the Conceptual Age requires adding another dimension for effective and efficient capital market governance.

Using the three-dimensional Rubik's Cube approach,[34] policymakers can mix-and-match individual cubes, irrespective of market scenarios and different beginning configurations. Events and competitive responses can be modeled for effective and efficient governance. To this point, Stanford mathematician Tomas Rokicki proved that any configuration of a Rubik's Cube can be solved in a maximum of 23 moves.

First, use the GAAMA model to monitor disproportionate governance inefficiencies that are subsidizing externalities, and then use the regulatory Rubik's Cube to determine the timing and sequence of economic remedies. Before you can think outside of the box, you first must think outside the square.

---

[33] Rubik's Cube® used by permission of Seven Towns Ltd., www.rubiks.com.
[34] Use an eight-cube model to test it before advancing to the 27-cube type.

PART V TAKEAWAYS

Market efficiency is a measure of the transactional cost, time, and effort to change ownership. The three-dimensional GAAMA model's feedback system monitors transactional Pareto efficiency.

Efficient markets exhibit a high degree of informational correlation to operational commands. A correlation coefficient measures the degree to which an issuer's stock price reacts to material market information.

Negatively correlated commands provide perverse incentives to subsidize externalities.

The changes in the level of economic activity are a series of small, normally distributed Gaussian changes. What varies is not so much the amount of commerce conducted as where it is conducted. Once economic activity attains a critical level of commerce, regulation does not stop, but merely specifies where the activity is likely to be conducted and how much it costs to conduct. Economic activity either going beyond or falling short of the normative operating range then creates externalities of controlled, offshore, balkanized, and underground markets.

Furthermore, a function is continuous if and only if it preserves the boundary of its limits. This is conditioned by not

- Misapplying tactics by using retrospective rules to plan
- Mischaracterizing the initial condition, resulting in a disproportionate level of commands to incentives
- Misspecifying commercial activity to conflate risk and uncertainty

Otherwise controlled, offshore, balkanized, or underground market externalities result because of spillover costs incurred when the producers and consumers in a market either do not bear all of the costs or do not reap all of the benefits of the market activity.[35]

To manage effectively and efficiently in the Conceptual Age, one must think in three dimensions.

The GAAMA model is a three-dimensional depiction of the interaction between normative and non-normative market externalities. Use the GAAMA model first to monitor disproportionate governance inefficiencies that are subsi-

---

[35] "Think Before You Regulate: Choose a Better Model," Stephen A. Boyko, *SFO Magazine*, May 2009.

dizing externalities. Follow with the regulatory Rubik's Cube to determine the timing and sequence of economic remedies.

Using 3-D Rubik's Cube approach, policymakers can mix and match individual cubes, irrespective of market scenarios and different beginning regulatory configurations.

Events and competitive responses can be modeled for effective and efficient governance. The Regulatory Rubik's Cube holds that regulation in the Conceptual Age requires adding another dimension for effective and efficient capital market governance.

J. Kyle Bass saw the profit potential in shorting the subprime bubble—a three-dimensional approach that earned him billions. Others saw only a two-dimensional circle and missed the opportunity. Global capital markets require three-dimensional decision-making capabilities. The growing policy shortcoming is that regulators govern with two-dimensional metrics in a three-dimensional world.

Bubbles are the antithesis of efficient. Efficient markets have IPOs priced on-the-margin to maximize profits. Bubbles create moral hazards, requiring government bailouts that are priced on-the-average to maximize safety-net coverage (a first class stamp sends your mail across the street or across the country for the same price).

Rent-seeking and free-riding agents of change create bubbles of self-organized criticality. Commentators have noticed that unsustainable bubbles in asset prices have become the mainstay of U.S. policymaking. Market bubbles are price distortions and emanate from two basic sources: too much paper currency, resulting in excess liquidity that overflows hard assets and is the result of bad fiscal and/or monetary policy; or the financial equivalent of pate de foie gras resulting from bad regulatory policy that immobilizes the flow of capital.

Be alert for the coming of a "green" economic bubble. How do I know? Let's review the **The Green Economic Bubble Boom Cycle**.

Introductory Phase: Reflexive demands and assumptions provide the foundation for the Gigaton Throwdown,[36] an initiative to encourage investors, entrepreneurs, business leaders, and policymakers to think big and massively scale

---

[36] The Gigaton Throwdown, San Francisco, California (gigatonthrowdown.org).

The Green Economic Bubble Boom Cycle

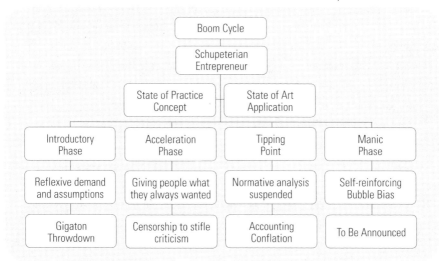

clean energy during the next 10 years. The goal is to remove a gigaton of carbon dioxide (1 billion tons) from the atmosphere.

"What we've outlined today is an ambitious goal, but one that is entirely attainable through hard work and a concerted effort between governments, business, and private investment," said Sunil Paul, founder of the Gigaton Throwdown and founding director of Spring Ventures.[37]

"This study is a loud, clear message about the importance of acting now to create a vibrant clean energy economy," said U.S. Senator John Kerry (D-Massachusetts). "By passing strong legislation, we can grow our economy and end our dependence on foreign oil. We can ensure that the United States takes back the lead in creating the clean energy technologies of the future—wind turbines, solar panels, and energy efficiency products—and that American companies benefit. This will help rebuild our manufacturing base, jump-start our economy, and create millions of clean energy jobs that can't be shipped overseas."[38]

Acceleration Phase: Earlier in the text, the crash phase of the bust cycle was profiled when people of influence spoke in undifferentiated terms. The contrapositive also holds, when people of influence censor critics who voice dissenting (differentiated) opinions.

---

[37] The Gigaton Throwdown, San Francisco, California (gigatonthrowdown.org).
[38] Ibid.

Consider this quote from Alan Carlin, senior analyst in the Environmental Protection Agency's National Center for Environmental Economics and a 35-year EPA veteran: "In March, the Obama EPA prepared to engage the global-warming debate in an astounding new way, by issuing an 'endangerment' finding on carbon. It establishes that carbon is a pollutant and thereby gives the EPA the authority to regulate it—even if Congress doesn't act."[39]

Carlin and a colleague presented their 98-page analysis arguing the EPA should take another look, as the science behind man-made global warming is inconclusive at best. The analysis noted that global temperatures were on a downward trend. It pointed out problems with climate models. It highlighted new research that contradicts apocalyptic scenarios. "We believe our concerns and reservations are sufficiently important to warrant a serious review of the science by EPA," read their report.

The response was an email to Carlin from his boss, Al McGartland, forbidding him from "any direct communication" with anyone outside his office regarding his analysis.

When Carlin tried again to disseminate his analysis, McGartland decreed: "The administrator and the administration have decided to move forward on endangerment, and your comments do not help the legal or policy case for this decision. ... I can only see one impact of your comments given where we are in the process, and that would be a very negative impact on our office."

McGartland blasted yet another email: "With the endangerment finding nearly final, you need to move on to other issues and subjects. I don't want you to spend any additional EPA time on climate change. No papers, no research etc., at least until we see what EPA is going to do with climate."[40]

Ideology? Nope, not here. Just us science folk. Honest.

Tipping Point: This occurs when normative analysis is suspended. The Random House College Dictionary defines **cost** as the price paid to produce, acquire, and/or maintain an asset. Missing in the definition is the cost of the price paid to remove the asset from societal use.

---

[39] The Gigaton Throwdown, San Francisco, California (gigatonthrowdown.org).
[40] "The EPA Silences a Climate Skeptic," Kimberley Strassel, *Wall Street Journal*, July 3, 2009.

For example, the United States generates a little more than 246 million tons of garbage per year, which is transferred to a landfill (50%); recycling facility (25%); or incinerator (25%). If the incineration fee of $65 per ton is used as a simple proxy for the cost to remove an asset from societal use and compared to the $35 per ton for landfill and recycling fees that represent a staged asset removal, a free-riding problem is created that is in excess of $5.4 billion.

It should be noted that due to a lack of descriptive precision that troubles much of the environmental movement, this effort has been hindered by the erroneous linking of financial self-sustainability with environmental operational sustainability.

Financial self-sustainability is a cash-flow stream limited to covering the variable margin. Environmental operational sustainability is long-term maintenance of ecosystem components and functions for future generations.

To the extent that eco-entrepreneurship advances environmentalism from financial self-sustainability to the higher goal of commercial viability (CV), it provides for a net-benefit return on capital, affording a broader societal scope. CV enables well-informed consumers to undergo an AIDA conversion to become stakeholders in a proportionate carbon-market governance regime.

George Soros observed that the former Soviet Union fell because it treated capital as a cost-free byproduct of a political process.[41] Care should be taken to ensure that the environmental movement avoids a similar mistake. Good intentions must be supported by good execution. Absent a proportionate carbon governance regime, how can society know it is pursuing a best path to achieve eco-sustainability? Without a transparent scoring system, how can society know a project is commercially viable to produce a net benefit or a green bubble?

Manic Phase: To be announced. Stay tuned. Anyone want to start a green hedge fund?

---

[41] "The EPA Silences a Climate Skeptic," Kimberley Strassel, *Wall Street Journal*, July 3, 2009.

PART SIX
A Better Way

SUMMARY ANALYSIS

It has taken nearly 50,000 words for me to explain that capital markets are the lifeblood of capitalism and why transformational governance innovation is needed.

Given *Boyko's Law of Inverse Relationship of Veritas to Verbosity*, the following disclosure should have come at the beginning, not the end:

- The Lord's Prayer: 71 words
- The 10 Commandments: 86 words
- The Gettysburg Address: 278 words
- The Declaration of Independence: 1,322 words
- U.S. government regulations on the sale of cabbage: 26,911 words
- U.S. Treasury's Financial Regulatory Reform: 42,897 words
- My take on capital market governance: 50,000 words

This does not negate the seriousness of the situation, given the frequency and size of financial bubbles and the amount of commerce being conducted in economic externalities. Companies turn to capital markets to raise the funds needed to finance the building of factories and office buildings; conduct research and development for innovation; and support a host of other essential corporate activities that create wealth and provide the highest standard of living in the world.

Currently, there is a lot of counterfactual reasoning put forth about the need for alternative solutions for market regulation. Of capitalism's critics I ask, what is your model for success? What is its track record? Where would you rather have been during the last 35 years?

But forget the communal negativity. If the economy and the market are as bad as the critics want us to believe, sell short. Why waste the time and the brainpower arguing about how to reposition the deck chairs on the Titanic? Have the courage of your convictions. That way you could put a smile on your face and put some money in the bank. You could even go to the bank singing the *Communist Internationale*:

Arise, wretched of the earth
Arise, convicts of hunger
Reason thunders in its crater
This is the eruption of the end
Of the past let us wipe the slate clean
Masses, slaves, arise, arise
The world is about to change its foundation
We are nothing, let us be all.

Comparison of
Governance and Rule-writing

GOVERNANCE: ORGANIZING PROCESS FOR CAPITAL MARKET DECISION MAKING	RULE WRITING: PROSCRIPTIVE DESCRIPTION OF AN ADVERSE MARKET CONDITION
Comprehensive problem solving	Proscriptive description
Randomness Predictable Probabilistic Indeterminate	Deterministic
Segmented: Cash flow and related information correlation	One-size-fits-all
3-D systemic knowledge	2-D commercial censorship
Market-driven net benefit	Rent-seeking protection cost

Not exactly "Be All You Can Be," but a real turn-on for the clinically depressed.

I have argued for comprehensive governance, not for more regulation that creates large, unresponsive oligopolies that compete through regulatory rule writing. Transformative governance enables the capital market to become more effective and more efficient. I have illustrated my points with original context and constructs, not comments on comments. Historical dots were connected in each chapter to create a unifying theme that provided several unique insights for section takeaways.

I am for competition, not commercial brinksmanship. I do not condone the misconduct of highly compensated Wall Street executives who were guilty of randomness mismanagement.

How do we make capital market governance more effective and efficient? Since most people know more about what they don't want rather than what they want, maybe it is best to start with a contrapositive argument of what capital market governance is not—rule writing.

As I have discussed, rule writing is the proscriptive description of an undesirable situation. It does not necessarily produce a net benefit and should not to be considered synonymous with governance. It doesn't fix anything.

SOX epitomizes rule writing. Why? SOX came about in reaction to a number of major corporate and accounting scandals. If it is as beneficial as its supporters claim, where has it been cited in SEC enforcement cases since its inception? Given the lack of actions against violators, it appears SOX's regulatory effect has been to push capital and innovation offshore.

At its core, SOX's regulatory efficacy is problematic; it mischaracterizes the initial condition by imposing remedies for firm maladies as systemic, market best practices. It is difficult for micro solutions intended for firms to withstand the macro, systemic stress testing of the market. Changing one element of the system changes the entire system. Why should the entire marketplace have to pay for the mistakes of the few?

Rule writing mischaracterizes the initial condition. There is a subtle but fundamental difference between natural disasters, stock market crashes (processes), and financial crises (events). Philosopher Jean-Jacques Rousseau first noted this difference in 1755, when an earthquake shook Portugal.

In a letter to Voltaire one year later, Rousseau noted that nature had not built [process] the houses that collapsed and suggested that Lisbon's high population density [process] contributed to the earthquake toll [event][1].

His point was that financial crises (i.e., Enron) are hazards that come from an outside agitator. Thus, these crises require tactical, procedural changes. Conversely, stock market crashes (i.e., subprime) result from endogenous systemic processes—those lacking an external cause. Crashes require strategic policy changes.

Misunderstanding the conditions and/or failing to become educated carries heavy consequences, such as the government-sanctioned free riding and rent seeking caused by rule writing.

It is ironic is that—having demonstrated the virtues of the capitalistic system—American policymakers are now trying to recreate the governance regime of European ancestry.

Napoleonic Code governs Europe, where an activity is prohibited unless expressly permitted. English Common Law reverses this process: Unless an activity is expressly prohibited, it is permitted.

---

[1] "Disaster Theory for Techies," Patrick Philippe Meier, *iRevolution*, May 15, 2009.

America is great because it took the English concept of "openness" and added "sweat equity" as an incentive to the settlers of the frontier. By equating risk and uncertainty, policymakers revert to the metrics of the Napoleonic Code, rendering SOX-type rules that are disproportionate for smaller issuers. Are our policymakers fostering what our ancestors rejected?[2]

Now let's go on offense to develop effective and efficient capital market governance. Effectiveness is must be established before addressing efficiency issues. It focuses on doing the right things by segmenting market randomness.

To develop effective comprehensive governance, we must segment the capital market into three governance regimes of randomness.

One regime for predictable money market instruments having predictable cash flow (i.e., "don't break the buck").

One regime for probabilistic, earnings-driven, large-cap issues having positive cash flow.

One regime for uncertain, event-driven, small-cap issues having negative cash flow.

Reflexive Financial and Operational (FINOP) analyses determine the effectiveness of capital market governance. The analysis deals with capital market bubbles, describing activities that led to market excesses and resultant errors of commission quantified in the cost of crashes.

FINOP analysis deals with the GAAMA model and the amount of commerce conducted in market externalities. It is the absence of activity resulting in errors of omission. By taking away future opportunity, the cost of potential errors of omission is incalculable at this time. The lost benefits and costs are uncertain.

Stock market crashes are social phenomena where external economic events combine with crowd behavior to form speculative, boom-bust bubbles. The term "Minsky Moment" is key to understanding the bubble's denouement—the financial market's bubble bursting.

Financial market fragility, in the normal life cycle of an economy, combines with the financial market's internal speculative investment bubbles. Minsky claimed excess corporate cash flow rises beyond what is needed during prosperous times. A speculative euphoria develops. This explains why bubbles go higher

---

[2] "How the SEC Impedes the Growth of Small Business," Stephen A. Boyko, *Yorktown Patriot*, May 26, 2006.

and last longer than logic suggests. At higher prices there are a greater number of intrepid investors who can pyramid speculative profits.

As long we have a right to choose, there will be bubbles. We need to learn how to better-manage bubbles. The classic example is Holland's "tulip mania," which dates to the first part of the 17th century.

Introduced to Europe a century earlier, tulips had become popular in Holland. A competition among the middle class to possess the rarest tulip—a status symbol—ensued.[3]

This bubble continued until prices reached unsustainable levels. By 1623, a single bulb of a famous tulip breed could cost as much as 1,000 florins (the average annual income was 150 florins).[4] It was also common to exchange tulips for land, livestock, and homes.

Legend has it a tulip trader could earn 60,000 florins per month. By 1635, it was recorded that 40 bulbs were sold for 100,000 florins.[5] (At the time, a ton of butter cost 100 florins, and eight fattened hogs cost 240.) A year later, tulips were traded on several Dutch stock exchanges, opening up the trade to a wider segment of society. Citizens sold other possessions to speculate in the tulip market,[6] and some made huge profits. Some sold recently planted bulbs or those they intended to plant—tulip futures—or as the Dutch called them, "wind trades."[7] (A state edict in 1610 had made wind trades illegal but failed to curtail the sales[8]—eerily similar to Fannie Mae's testimony before the House of Representatives banking committee.)

Air began to seep from the bubble in 1637, when traders couldn't get inflated prices for bulbs. They began selling and the bubble burst. Panic selling spread. Buyers were stuck with contracts to purchase tulips at now ridiculous prices, while others possessed relatively worthless bulbs. Thousands of merchants and nobles were ruined financially, as courts refused to enforce payment contracts; judges regarded the debts as "gambling."[9]

---

[3] Dash, Mike. *Tulipomania: The Story of the World's Most Coveted Flower and the Extraordinary Passions it Aroused,"* Three Rivers Press, New York, N.Y., 2001) p. 110-180.
[4] Ibid.
[5] Ibid.
[6] Ibid.
[7] Ibid.
[8] Ibid.
[9] Ibid.

Regulators create governance regimes by choosing appropriate commands for the set of available economic incentives. This balances command costs attendant to shareholder rights with incentive benefits derived from shareholder responsibilities. Otherwise, providing rights in excess of responsibilities degenerates to unlegislated subsidies, which oftentimes spawn economic bubbles. Bubbles are antithetical to market effectiveness and efficiency.

The three-dimensional GAAMA model depicts the operational interaction of normative and non-normative controlled, offshore, balkanized, and underground market externalities. It is a diagnostic tool for measuring the degree of societal compliance with the established governance.

The vertical y-axis represents qualitative standards; the horizontal x-axis represents quantitative rules; and the perpendicular z-axis represents the relationship between available economic incentives and commands. What varies is not so much the amount of commerce conducted as where it is conducted.

Once economic activity attains a critical level of commerce, regulation does not stop it from happening. It merely specifies where the activity is likely conducted and how much it costs to conduct. Economic activity either beyond or short of the normative operating range then creates externalities of controlled, offshore, balkanized, or underground markets.

Efficiency is the processes for reflexively managing the dynamic governance forces of societal stability and societal change that focuses on doing things right. Efficiency is a measure of time, cost, and effort.

Reflexive FINOP analyses also serve to determine the efficiency of capital market governance.

Efficient markets exhibit a high degree of informational correlation to financial cash flow. A correlation coefficient is a measure of the degree to which an issuer's stock price reacts to material market information. The value of the correlation coefficient ranges from -1 to +1. A value of +1 indicates perfect positive correlation, with prices moving simultaneously in the same direction and magnitude. A correlation coefficient of -1 indicates perfect negative correlation, with prices moving simultaneously in opposite directions and magnitude. A correlation coefficient of 0 indicates there is no relationship.

Negatively correlated commands provide perverse incentives to subsidize externalities.

Alterations in the level of economic activity are a series of small, normally distributed Gaussian changes. Again, what varies is not so much the amount of commerce conducted as where it is conducted. Once economic activity attains a critical level of commerce, regulation does not stop, but merely specifies where the activity is likely conducted and how much it costs to conduct.

Operationally, the GAAMA model indicates that economic activity either beyond or short of the normative operating range then creates externalities of controlled, offshore, balkanized, or underground markets.

To manage efficiently in the Conceptual Age, one must think in three dimensions. Use the GAAMA model first to monitor disproportionate governance inefficiencies that subsidize externalities. You can then use the regulatory Rubik's Cube to determine the timing and sequence of economic remedies.

Global capital markets require three-dimensional decision-making capabilities. The growing policy shortcoming is that regulators govern with two-dimensional metrics—the opposite of efficient.

Better management of the normative market is essential for the requisite economic growth and wealth creation needed to provide a societal net benefit. This minimizes the adverse effects of economic bubbles and externalities.

It also is the best argument against claims that capital market practitioners are "unethical" and "greedy." Such descriptions illustrate a fundamental lack of definitional completeness, clarity, and congruency.

Quite often, ethics is defined incorrectly, based on personal feelings or societal perceptions about right and wrong. In reality, ethics is the moral domain beyond legal compliance—a shingle theory implying a market practitioner's fiduciary responsibility to conduct business in accordance with just and equitable principles of fair trade.

The shingle theory is the dependent variable in support of the cited principle and rule. Both constructs and contexts are necessary for effective and efficient governance. In the absence of a method for determining rule violations, ethical context too often becomes subjective and too quickly degenerates to the moral equivalent of rule writing.

Post-subprime bubble judgment is broaching the threshold that "failure equals fraud." Home ownership is a positive societal goal. But NINJA loans gave property rights to renters. Where were the ethical boundaries for securitizing negative equity mortgages structured at the behest of Fannie Mae's mission to increase home ownership pursuant to the CRA? The answer lies more with market metrics than morals.

Ethical allegations require a governance structure from which to opine. The absence of such structure results in relativistic revisionism totally dependent on financial results. The underlying, uncertain economic environment for securitized negative equity mortgages and for securitized negative cash flow mortgages is in conflict with the deterministic, one-size-fits-all governance regime. This lack of disclosure frustrates the market's price discovery function. It borders on entrapment, where the last practitioner in the sequence of events becomes the aggregator of liability.

The socialistic sophistry with regard to capitalistic "greed" is illustrated by an October 2008 *Los Angeles Times* editorial, which concluded "low-income borrowers and affordable-housing advocates didn't cause the credit crisis. The real villains were greedy mortgage brokers, lenders, and investors."[10]

In the absence of compliance allegations, how is the *Times* argument plausible in an environment where shareholder rights equal shareholder responsibilities? If there are allegations of wrongdoing, submit the evidence. If there is an imbalance of shareholder rights relative to shareholder responsibilities, stipulate the free-riding and/or rent-seeking subsidy.

The newspaper's argument hinges on this statement:

> "At first the focus was on greedy profiteers among lenders and investment bankers, who were an easy (and deserving) target. Then the finger pointing became politicized, with Democrats blaming deregulation advocates in the Bush administration and previous GOP-controlled Congresses, and Republicans citing influential Democrats at Fannie Mae and Freddie Mac and their allies on Capitol Hill. … Borrowers made their share of mistakes and reckless decisions, but the more fundamental problem is that too many mortgage brokers, lenders, and investors stopped caring whether loans could be repaid. They abandoned the underwriting standards that would have protected borrowers and lenders alike."[11]

Greed is the sour grape argument given when financial creativity does not produce the advertised cash flow and rate of return. If, as the *Times* editorial claims, "the last thing anyone wanted from the CRA were the exotic mortgages that have failed at alarming rates,"[12]

---

[10] "Suprime Meltdown Culprits," *Los Angeles Times*, October 25, 2008.
[11] Ibid.
[12] Ibid.

does not the same logic apply to the financial provider? Those providers were investors, not landlords. The *Times* contends there is so much money to be made from the subprime market. If so, why would anyone make goose soup from the Golden Goose?

The editorial indicates a basic misconception about the nature of markets as dynamic, nonlinear systems. *Dynamic* indicates change, and *nonlinear* suggests that inputs may not be equal to outputs. How does a person on salary evaluate the productivity of an employee on commission?

Whenever someone degenerates to using *ad hominem* attacks, it suggests they are out of intellectual bullets. Their worldview is threatened, and they are reduced name-calling criticisms, in lieu of constructive enhancements. Where were suggestions for underwriting effective and efficient low-to-moderate income mortgages?

This book is a little step toward improving the capital market through better governance, not more rules. Progress will require innovative, knowledge-driven adaptations. If we don't make the necessary changes, our capital market will be caught in a recursive loop of errors and omission. Such inefficiencies will eventually render our source of economic wealth ineffective. Then we're *all* screwed.

GLOSSARY

Affinity scam: swindle that targets a particular group, based on distinctive traits perpetrators share with the group

Apparatchick: derogatory term for an official who is part of a large organization or political party

ABS: asset-backed security; financial instrument that derives value and income from a specified asset(s)

Asset lite: the combination of small investments in a capital-intensive industry, derivatives trading, and market making

AIDA: stands for "awareness," "interest," "desire" and "action"; strategy based on differentiated marketing

Balkanized: to be divided into smaller units, which are often hostile toward each other; occurs in markets where low standards interact with too few best-practice operating rules for a given level of commercial activity

Bear market: prolonged period of falling prices and general, widespread pessimism

Black swan: symbol based on the ancient Western belief that all swans are white; intended to reference the improbable

Boom-bust bubble: a boom, or period of growth, creates a bubble when SOP technologies, goods, or products integrate with SOA applications, thus generating profit for early adapters; the bust is a dramatic drop in prices; a bubble is definitively characterized only after prices crash

Bull market: a prolonged period in which prices rise faster than the historical average; result from periods of unprecedented innovation, economic recovery, and other economic booms

Capitalization: a company's market price, calculated by multiplying number of shares outstanding by the price per share

Cash flow: measures of financial health calculating net income plus non-cash charges

Change: the relationship between risk and uncertainty

Chaos Theory: describes nature of systems as they evolve and exhibit dynamics that are highly sensitive to initial conditions; applies to mathematics, physics, and natural systems

Circuit breakers: pause in trading at specified price points, allowing the market to "break cadence" and give investors time to assimilate incoming information; gives investors the ability to make informed choices during periods of high market volatility without falling victim to herd behavior; approved by SEC in 1998

Classical economics: ideology favoring free trade and laissez-faire, or "hands off," governance; began in 1776 with Adam Smith's The Wealth of Nations

Clawbacks: money or benefit revoked due to special circumstances; retraction of stock prices or market

CDO: collateralized debt obligations; type of structured asset-backed security that derives value and payments from a portfolio of fixed-income underlying assets

Complexity Theory: concerned with the prolonged behavior of certain kinds of complex systems; under certain conditions the systems perform in regular, predictable ways and under other conditions, the systems exhibit irregular and unpredictable behavior; almost undetectable differences in initial conditions lead to gradually diverging system reactions until eventually the evolution of behavior is quite dissimilar.

Comprehensive governance: based on codified best practices; provides a societal net benefit in terms of greater wealth to an expanding investor base; accounts for randomness; emphasizes investor education; reduces the number of noise traders with shareholder rights proportionate to shareholder responsibilities

CFPA: Consumer Financial Protection Agency; organization proposed in the U.S. Treasury's Financial Regulatory Reform

CLS: Continuous Linked Settlement; created in September 2002 by several of the world's largest banks for the purpose of settling foreign exchange flows amongst themselves

Correlation coefficient: a measure of the degree to which an issuer's stock price reacts to material market information

Crash: social phenomena where external economic events combine with crowd behavior to form speculative, sudden, dramatic, double-digit decline in stock prices; results in broad-based decline measured across a significant section of a stock market

Creative destruction: practice of perturbing Walrasian equilibrium with transformative societal innovations to force adoption of new patterns of production and consumption

Crisis: catastrophic, issue-specific financial loss resulting from a particular event or institution; does not affect the majority of market investors

Data mining: practice using information extraction techniques to accumulate and separate facts from assumptions; correlates facts to format recognizable information patterns

Determinate economic environment: limited or determined

Disintermediate: occurs when investors transfer their funds to other economic instruments because they believe conventional economic methods do not pay sufficient interest to keep pace with inflation; generally leads to a rapid growth in the alternate instruments and a loss from traditional institutions, such as savings banks

DJIA: Dow Jones Industrial Average

EBITDA: earnings before interest, taxes, depreciation, and amortizationEconomists of change: the economic drivers of the boom-bust cycle, feeding the boom through "creative destruction"; those whose thinking aligns with the perspectives of economist Joseph Schumpeter and Post-Keynesians

Economies of scale: environment where unit production cost decreases as the number of goods produced increases

Economies of scope: environment where unit production costs decrease as variety of goods produced increase

Economies of span: environment where decreased transaction costs between stages of production and per-unit costs decline

Economies of speed: achieved by using an asset to produce outputs at a higher rate of throughput.

Elements: one of categories in Popper's D-N model; identifies initial conditions, final conditions, and universally valid generalizations

Enforcement: the tactical application of regulatory principles and rules

Entrepreneurs: commercial agents of change; conceptual problem solvers who fulfill unmet needs; innovators of new products, new processes, and new markets; viewed by economist Joseph Schumpeter as disturbers of economic equilibrium and the cause of economic development

EntEx: Entrepreneur Exchange; Boyko's proposed micro-cap market, with a governance approach specifically tailored for indeterminate SMEs

ETFs: exchange-traded funds

Explanation: one of three operations noted in Popper's D-N model; combines final conditions with universally valid generalizations

Externality: spillover of an economic transaction; OTC derivative markets; can cause market failure if the price mechanism does not account for the full social costs and benefits of production and consumption

FLITE model: evaluates the fairness, liquidity, integration, transparency, and efficiency of a market; defined in terms of number of people affected by the command and relative importance of the command

The Fed: Federal Reserve System; the central bank of the United States

FASB 157: Financial Accounting Standards Board Number 157; defines fair value; establishes a framework for measuring fair value in GAAP;

expands disclosures about fair value measurements

FINRA: Financial Industry Regulatory Authority; the largest independent securities regulator in the United States

FIRREA: Financial Institutions Reform Recovery and Enforcement Act of 1989; provided $50 billion to close failed banks and stop further losses; resulted in the formation of RTC

Financial pro forma: financial statements prepared prior to a planned transaction; anticipates results of the transaction's projected cash flows, net revenues and possible taxes

Financial Regulatory Reform: regulatory proposal released in 2009 by the U.S. Department of The Treasury

Firms: non-market entities that shift the cost burden in favor of competitive advantage; economic actors that transform inputs to outputs for use by other economic agents; organized to perform integrated functions that might otherwise be outsourced to a competitive marketplace; tend to be closed in function and vertical in structure when they reach maturity

Free cash flow: measures of financial health calculating cash flow minus contractual commitments and capital budgeting systems

Fuzzy attractors: explains the formation of a fuzzy subset of the state of space; from Complexity Theory

GAAP: generally accepted accounting principles

Glass-Steagall Act of 1933 (GSA): established the Federal Deposit Insurance Corporation and other banking reforms in response to the Great Depression; did not change unit banking within states or the ban on nationwide banking; prohibitions preventing bank holding companies from owning other financial companies were repealed by the Gramm-Leach-Bliley Act of 1999, which superseded much of GSA

Gosplan: The Soviet Union's State Planning Committee; responsible for nationwide economic planning via five-year plans; under the direction of the Communist Party

Governance: commercial problem-solving process designed to maximize stakeholder value; the set of processes, customs, policies, laws, and institutions affecting the way an enterprise is directed, administered, and controlled; the relationships among stakeholders and the goals by which stakeholders assert their rights through an elected board of directors and management; a system of checks and balances designed to ensure managers are vigilant on behalf of long-term stakeholder value
Granularity: the degree of precision required for compliance
Gravitas: the seriousness of a violation, as measured by the amount of a fine or punishment
Gresham's Law: bad money drives good money out of circulation as people hoard the valued currency
GDP: gross domestic product; market value of all a nation's goods and services made within a year's time; basic measure of a nation's economic performance
Group-think: to go along with the popular opinion—usually the boss's—to protect yourself, your job, and your interests
Indeterminate economic environment: unlimited, undefined, vague
Indeterminate issuers: enterprises that focus on managing their burn rate; associated with negative cash flow
Indeterminism: philosophy based on the idea that because people have free will, their actions cannot always be accurately predicted based on past behavior and events
Infomediation: products and/or resources that make it easier to get information related to transactional processes
Intermediaries: those who provide sponsorship to compensate for uncertainty, relative to a lack of product information and/or a lack of niche market efficiencies
Intermediation: process in which a bank or other outside party brings together a lender and borrower in exchange for a small return

IPO: initial public offering; occurs when a company issues stock or shares to the public for the first time

Invisible hand: refers to the marketplace's ability to regulate itself; coined by Adam Smith in *The Wealth of Nations* (1776)

Junior tranches: those that offer higher coupon payments or lower prices to compensate for additional default risk

Keynesian economics: ideology that advocates government spending to increase aggregate demand; named for John Maynard Keynes, author of *General Theory of Employment, Interest and Money* (1936); denies the concept of the "invisible hand," as set forth by economist Adam Smith; evolved into Neoclassical Keynesian and Post-Keynesian economics

Large-cap issuers: Companies with $10 billion to $200 billion capitalization

Legacy governance: doing things the way they have always been done because that is the way they have always been done

Liquidity: state in which there are sufficient buyers and sellers to consummate transactions at prices reasonably related to quoted market prices; a function of time, volatility, depth, breadth, and the resiliency of the marketplace

Market: coordinated, nonlinear, dynamic pricing system that allocates voluntary exchanges between consumers, workers, and owners of production; open in function and horizontal in structure until reaching maturity

Market evolution: process by which information correlates into predictable, probabilistic, and uncertain regimes based on the underlying economic environment's degree of randomness; process by which markets self-select efficient development pathways to minimize competitive advantage based on market knowledge

Market segmentation: subdividing a market along a self-referential or common ground; concentrates marketing energy and force on the targeted segment to gain a competitive advantage

Mass market: the largest group of consumers who wish to buy a product

Matrix problem analysis: compares and contrasts similar byproduct solutions that are essential to understanding the problem of suboptimal governance; makes connection between too low standards for information correlation and ineffective strategy results

Mid-cap issuers: Companies with $2 billion to $10 billion capitalization

Minsky Moment: the point at which a major selloff begins because no counter party can be found to bid at the high, quoted prices; occurs when investors have cash flow problems due to spiraling debt, resulting from financing speculative investments; term was coined by Paul McCulley of PIMCO; named for economist Hyman Minsky

MILD technique: problem-analysis method comparing and contrasting results from modeling (mathematics, matrices, and physical representations), investigation (brainstorming and reverse engineering), logic (decision tree and "If I do X, then Y will happen" reasoning), and data mining

Monetarism: economic ideology stressing the primary importance of money supply in determining nominal GDP and price level; founded upon classical assumptions of market efficiency; advocates rational expectations; suggests governmental attempts to control the economy are doomed because economic actors could easily game the outcome; based on the work of economist Milton Friedman

NASDAQ: National Association of Securities Dealers Automated Quotations; the largest electronic, screen-based equity securities trading market in the United States; handles more trading volume per hour than any other stock exchange worldwide

Neoclassical Keynesian: ideology that takes insights from Keynes and the general framework of classical economics; belief in the economics of imperfection—price inflexibility and informational asymmetries; influenced by economist Joseph Stiglitz

Net Capital Rule: requirement that broker-dealers have sufficient liquid assets, enabling firms that fall below minimum requirements to liquidate quickly

NYSE: New York Stock Exchange; with Euronext, operates the world's largest and most liquid exchange group
Niche market: a division of the market focused sale of a specific product(s) or service(s)
Nodes: individual actors within networks
Nomenklatura: elite group or class from which candidates and appointees for top-level positions are selected, especially in politics
Operating cash flow: measures of financial health calculating earnings before taxes plus non-cash charges (EBITDA)
Pareto optimality: situation where change cannot make anyone better off without sacrificing the well being of another before economists can say it is unambiguously better; named for Italian economist Vilfredo Pareto
Pillared-risk outcome assessments: tests that identify, characterize, and understand risk, relative to alternative strategies; decision-making process often involving cost-benefit analysis, assessment of risk tolerance, and quantification of preference outcomes
Pink Sheets: the centralized quoting system for OTC trading; companies quoted on the Pink Sheets need not meet minimum requirements or file with the SEC
Popper's D-N model: deductive-nomological model with three elements, three operations, and three logical observations; scientific explanation in natural language that evaluates deductive arguments; posited in Karl Popper's Logic of Scientific Discovery (1934)
Popper's three operations: in Popper's D-N model, operations are prediction, explanation, and testing **Post-Keynesian:** ideology based primarily on the principle that demand is important in the long and short terms and creates a competitive economy that will not naturally achieve full employment

Predictability: logically expected

Prediction: one of the three operations noted in Popper's D-N model; combines initial conditions with universally valid generalizations.

Predictive solution: an equation or set of rules that makes it possible to forecast an unseen or unmeasured discrete value (the dependent variable or output) from other known values (independent variables or inputs)

Probability: likely or probable

Problem: measured observance outside a normative operating zone; causes deviation from course or plan

Prospective time perspective: focuses on something that is likely to happen in the future

Protection: the false notion that a regulatory agency can shelter investors from the risk and uncertainty that exists in capital markets

Randomness: process describing the probability of a factor being chosen within a range of 0%, or indeterminateness, to 100%, or predictive certainty; recognition and attendant disclosure of the prevailing economic environment is the foundation that drives governance for either determinate or indeterminate regimes

RTGS: real time gross settlement; system created by CLS in which both processing and final settlement of funds transfer instructions take place continuously to minimize asynchronous time lag risks

Relationship-based governance: small-scale environment in which a wide community of expert advisers, brokers, accountants, lawyers, and public relations firms creates a trading system with lower fixed costs but higher variable costs; works well in an indeterminate economic environment with early-stage public companies

Rent seekers: economic actors who manipulate the economic and/or legal environment; generally associated with government regulation and misuse of governmental authority, when rent seekers claiming to protect investors extract uncompensated value from unappropriated resources without making a commensurate contribution

RTC: Resolution Trust Corporation; government agency resulting from FIRREA; resold S&L assets and used the proceeds to pay back depositors; changed S&L regulations to improve price-discovery investment guidelines for loan originations

Retrospective time perspective: focus on past conditions to predict future outcomes

Risk: chance of loss; has foreseeable consequences

Rule writing: occurs when proscriptive description of an undesirable event or process produces a narrow-minded description of an undesirable situation; assumes societal buy-in by admonishing the public not to engage in a described undesirable practice; is not synonymous with "governance"

SOX: Sarbanes-Oxley Act of 2002; set new or enhanced standards for all U.S. publicly held company boards, management, and public accounting firms; contains 11 titles, or sections, ranging from additional corporate board responsibilities to criminal penalties, and requires the SEC to implement rulings on requirements to comply with the law

Scale: measure of size

Scope: breadth or range of product offerings

SEC: Securities Exchange Commission; agency of the U.S. government charged with enforcing federal securities laws and regulating financial exchanges and all securities markets

Senior tranches: safest securities; interest and principal payments are made in order of seniority

Settlement risk: occurs between the trade execution and settlement when there is a counter-party default in delivering a security or its value in cash

Span: coordination of sequence and timing of production

Speed: rate of throughput

SOA: state of the art; highest level of development for a good or service

SOP: state of practice; highest level of practice in delivering a good or service

Shingle theory: the idea that a broker who "hangs out a shingle" will treat customers responsibly and fairly when giving advice; introduced by the SEC in the 1930s

Six Sigma: developed by General Electric, it is a highly disciplined process focused on product development and delivery; it focuses on measuring and eliminating defects to reach a state of zero product defects; to achieve Six Sigma Quality, a product must produce no more than 3.4 defects per million opportunities

SMEs: small- and medium-sized enterprises

Small-cap issuers: Companies with $200 million to $2 billion capitalization

Testing: one of the three operations noted in Popper's D-N model; compares initial conditions to final conditions

Three-dimensional governance: governance model combining measurable conditions (minimum capital requirement), qualitative criteria (liquidity), and beneficial relationships (degree of connectedness)

Ties: relationships between participants within networks

Tranches: pieces or portions of structured financing, as divided into risk classes

Transaction cost: the framework for predicting when certain economic tasks are performed by firms and when they are performed on the market

Uncertainty: difficult, unusual circumstances; indeterminate situation with unforeseeable consequences; not a linear, riskier extension of "risk"

Walrasian equilibrium: the state in which each agent makes optimal choices, commensurate with his or her budget, and if an agent prefers another combination of goods, he or she cannot afford it; based on the theory developed by French economist Leon Walras

Welfare economics: economic study focused on individual wealth and comfort

INDEX

A

Affinity scam, 35
Agricultural Age, 140
Alternative Investment Market/AIM, 52-53, 80-81, 148-149, 150
Aristotle, 100
Prior Analytics, 100
William B. Arthur, 54
Asset-backed security/ABS, 96, 123
Asset lite, 32, 34
Asymmetrical information, 11, 12, 15, 16, 18, 33, 42, 51
Australian Small Scale Offerings Board/ASSOB, 149
AIDA, 108, 115, 157

B

Back-office processing, 22
Sheila Bair, 146
Per Bak, 98
Bailout, 23, 25, 131, 146, 154
Balkanized, 88, 127, 138, 143, 142, 149-150
Bank of America Corp., 38
J. Kyle Bass, 38, 154
Bear market, 4, 22, 37
Best practice, 30, 44-45, 50, 52, 56, 66, 104, 143
Black swan, 85, 99-100
Henry Blodget, 30
Boom, 9, 10, 16, 17, 28, 29, 36, 27, 155
Broughton Bridge collapse, 24
Bubble, 8, 10, 11, 19, 31, 37, 42, 129, 130, 154, 157, 160, 163-164, 166
Warren Buffett, 96, 123
George W. Bush, 9, 36, 167
Bust, 9, 10, 11, 17, 29, 31, 37, 39, 155, 163

C

Gene Callahan, 103
Capital/stock market, ix, 2, 3, 5, 6, 10, 12, 13, 14, 15, 17, 18, 19, 20, 21, 22, 23, 27, 44, 52, 57, 60, 72, 73, 88, 90, 93, 97, 99, 106-107, 109, 114, 117, 123, 126, 128, 130, 134, 141, 154, 160-161, 166, 168
Capitalism, 57, 104, 137, 160, 162, 167
Alan Carlin, 156
James Carter, 25
Change, 7-8, 11, 17, 30, 39-40, 44, 60, 61, 62-63, 81, 82, 93, 96-97, 98, 121, 126, 127, 129-130, 134, 135-138, 141, 148, 150, 154, 162, 165, 168
Chaos Theory, 98, 107, 130
S.J. Choi and A.C. Pritchard, 81
Circuit breakers, 21, 24, 37
Classical Economics, 11, 13, 14, 16, 18-19, 116
Ronald Coase, 107-108
The Nature of the Firm, 108
Collateralized debt obligation/CDO, 96, 123
Commands, 40, 44, 48, 52, 68, 69, 72, 77, 90, 106, 126, 128, 129, 141-142, 153, 165
Commercial viability/CV, 157
Community Reinvestment Act/CRA, 36, 85
Competition, 13, 18, 85, 129, 133, 141, 142, 146, 161, 164
Complexity Theory, 5, 29
Conceptual Age, 141, 152, 154, 166
Congress,
Consumer Financial Protection Agency/CFPA, 65, 82, 83, 84-85, 92

Continuous Linked Settlement/CLS, 21, 22
Crash, 4, 7, 8, 9, 10, 11, 13, 16, 17, 19, 20-21, 22-25, 99-100, 101-102, 130, 162, 163
Creative destruction, 17, 18, 137
Crisis, 7, 8, 9, 20, 21-22, 44, 65, 66, 67, 73, 79, 81-82, 86, 98, 99, 100, 106, 121, 123, 162
James Crotty, 17, 29

D

Data mining, 49
Debt, 17, 19, 33, 34, 36, 75, 97, 114, 133, 164
Department of Homeland Security, 98
Depository Institutions Deregulation and Monetary Control Act,
Hernando DeSoto, 71-72
Jamie Dimon, 60, 61, 146
Disintermediate, 88
Dislocation, 19, 21, 56, 74, 90, 91, 110
Dot-com bubble/boom, 28, 29, 32, 117
Dot-com crash, 21, 30, 31, 68
Dow Jones Industrial Average/DJIA, 2, 3, 4, 21, 23-24

E

Eco-entrepreneurship, 157
Economies of Scale, 18, 61, 89, 146
The Economist, 18, 61, 89, 146
Effective and efficient governance universe/EEGU, 109
Efficiency, 25-26, 52, 69, 70, 82, 90-91, 96, 126, 127, 128, 129, 132, 153, 163, 165
Efficient governance universe/EGU, 126, 127
Albert Einstein, 122-123
Enforcement, 33, 35, 68, 69-70, 82, 87, 92, 127, 161-162
English Common Law, 57, 162
Enron, 9, 15, 21, 32-34, 40, 68, 72
Entrepreneur, 17, 18, 28, 36, 63, 85, 96, 116, 127, 134, 136, 137, 138, 151, 154, 155

Entrepreneur Exchange/EntEX, 96, 102, 117, 118-121, 124, 126, 150, 152
National Center for Environmental Economics, 156
Ethernet, 6
E*trade, 30, 31
Equilibrium, 14, 18, 63, 107, 116, 142, 143
Externality, 52, 69, 72, 102, 103, 104, 127, 128, 138, 139, 143, 144, 145, 146, 153-154, 160, 163, 165, 166

F

FLITE model, 69, 107, 122
Eugene Fama, 13
Federal Deposit Insurance Corporation/FDIC, 7
Federal National Mortgage Corporation, 63
Fannie Mae, 130, 131, 134, 164, 166, 167
Freddie Mac, 130, 167
Federal Reserve/Fed, 4, 16, 20, 31, 66, 71, 73, 76, 77, 86
Regulation Q, 27
Finder, 150
Financial Accounting Standards Board/FASB, 38, 39, 55, 90-91
FASB 157, 21, 38, 39, 55, 90-91, 104
Financial Industry Regulatory Authority/FINRA, ix, 111, 112
National Association of Securities Dealers/NASD, ix, 134
Financial Institutions Reform Recovery and Enforcement Act/FIRREA, 25
Financial and operational/FINOP analysis, ix, 108, 133, 162, 163, 165
Firm, 15, 40, 76, 86
Mike Fletcher, 53
Forbearance, 26
Barney Frank, 57
Milton Friedman, 16, 76
Futures exchange, 23
Fuzzy attractor, 9

G
Timothy Geithner, 60
General Electric, 55, 85
Gigaton Throwdown, 154-156
Glass-Steagall Act/GSA, 7-8, 39-40
Global, asynchronous, asymmetrical, market activity/GAAMA model, 126, 127, 131, 138-139, 141, 143-144, 145, 152, 153, 165, 166
Global economy, 53, 141
Goodbody, 22-23
Google, 31, 32
Al Gore, 29
Gosplan, 57, 74
Governance, ix, 2, 7, 14, 15, 39-40, 44-45, 46, 50-51, 52, 53, 54, 57, 60, 61, 62-63, 68, 69, 96, 97, 102, 103, 104, 109, 110, 114, 118, 122, 126-128, 129, 133, 135, 136, 138, 140-141, 142, 161-163
Government-sponsored enterprise/GSE, 63, 106, 130, 132, 134
Gramm-Leach-Bliley Act, 7
Granularity, 69
Gravitas, 69
Great Depression, 65, 67
Alan Greenspan, 20
Gresham's law, 10

H
Iwan David Herstatt, 9, 22
Herstatt Bank of Cologne, 7, 21, 22, 68

I
Incentives, 22-23, 40, 44, 46, 53, 57, 69, 77, 102, 127, 128, 141-142, 143, 144
Indeterminism, 17
Industrial Age, 62, 140, 141
Industrial policy regime, 127, 132, 133, 134
Inflection point, 10, 31, 56
Infomediation, 41, 84, 109
Information Age, 62, 140, 41
Information superhighway, 28, 29
Intermediation, 84, 107
Internet, 10, 28, 30
Initial public offering/IPO, 28, 31, 50, 78, 117-118, 148-149, 154
Intrapreneur, 127, 136
Invisible hand, 14, 16, 78, 84

J
J. P. Morgan Chase & Co., 60

K
Jonathan G. Katz, 51, 63
George Kaufman, 25-26
John Maynard Keynes, 16, 18-19
   General Theory of Employment, Interest, and Money, 16
Keynesian Economics, 17
Robert Khuzami, 35, 91, 93, 94
Charles Kindleberger, 8, 18, 19
Frank H. Knight, 44-45, 104-105
   Risk, Uncertainty, and Profit, 44-45, 104-105

L
Large capital/cap, 12, 71-72, 109, 118, 126, 127
Law of Comparative Advantage, 147
Arthur Levitt, 71
Kenneth Lewis, 38-39
Stan Liebowitz, 101-102, 123
London Stock Exchange, 52, 80, 148
Long-Term Capital Management/LTCM, 9, 27-28, 40, 68, 73

M
Bernard L. Madoff, 8, 9, 21, 34-35, 42, 51, 68, 70-71, 92-93
   Bernard L. Madoff Investment Securities LLC, 34-35
Harry Markopolos, 35, 42, 92-93
Harry Markowitz, 110
Matrix analysis, 49, 50
McDash Analytics, 101
Bethany McLean, 33
Paul McCulley, 19
Merrill Lynch, 22-23, 30, 38, 62, 72, 146
John Meriwether, 27
Robert Merton, 27
Robert Metcalfe, 6

Metcalfe's law, 6
Metcalfe network, 6, 8, 115
Micro capital/cap, 115, 117-119, 120, 129
Merton Miller, 65
Hyman Minsky, 17, 18, 19, 34, 75, 163-164
Minsky Moment, 9, 17, 19, 30-31, 38, 97, 102, 130, 163
MILD technique, 48-49
Monetarism, 14-15, 16
Monetary policy, 16, 19
Money supply, 20
Monopoly, 44, 81
Mortgage-backed securities, 36, 38
Daniel H. Mudd, 130-131

N
Napoleonic Code, 57, 162-163
National Association of Securities Dealers Automated Quotations/NASDAQ, ix, 9, 30, 34, 62-63, 102, 115, 148, 149
National Clearing Corporation, 22
Negative cash-flow issuers, 102
Neoclassical Keynesian, 12, 16-17, 70
Net Capital Rule, 69, 111, 112, 143
New York Stock Exchange/NYSE, 2, 21, 22-23, 62-63, 102, 115, 117
Rule 80B, 24
1974 crash, 2, 4, 7, 21, 22
1987 crash, 4, 20-21, 23-24, 56, 68, 100, 123
NINJA/LIAR loans, 36, 38, 41, 57, 101, 123, 166
Noise trader, 10, 52, 104, 129
Non-normative market, 139, 144, 153
Normative market, 126-127, 138, 143, 144, 147, 166
No-to-Know/N2K, 62

O
Barack Obama, 66, 67, 146, 156
Office of Thrift Supervision/OTS, 65
Oligopoly, 18, 141, 142, 146, 148, 161
Over-the-counter/OTC derivatives, 60, 79, 103

OTC Bulletin Board, 115

P
Paper-crunch disaster, 23
Vilfredo Pareto, 103, 126
Pareto optimality/efficiency, 103, 104, 126, 129-130, 153
Hank Paulson, 39, 106
PFTS, 89
A.C. Pigou, 103-104
PIMCO, 19
Pink Sheets, 115
Ponzi scheme, 8, 34, 93
  Ponzi borrower, 17, 34, 75
Karl Raimund Popper, 63, 64
Popper's D-N model, 63, 64, 65, 67-68, 71-72, 89-90
Post-Keynesian Economics, 12, 17, 18019
P/E ratio, 46
Problem, 45-48, 55
Problem solving, 46-48, 50, 51, 54
Protection, 70-71, 82-83, 92, 109, 128, 147

Q
Quantity Theory of Money, 16

R
Radio Corporation of America/RCA, 5
Real Time Gross Settlement/RTGS, 21, 22
Reed's law, 6
Regulation, ix, 15, 25-26, 40, 44, 50, 51-52, 60, 66, 67-68, 70, 73-74, 76-77, 79, 85, 87-88, 90, 91, 92, 104-106, 109, 112, 156,
Regulatory Rubik's Cube®, 140, 152, 154
Rent seeking/free riding, 51, 52, 53, 69, 70, 83, 127, 129-130, 154, 161, 162, 167
Resolution Trust Corporation/RTC, 21, 25, 105

Risk, 22, 26, 28-29, 31, 40-41, 44-45, 51, 55, 60-61
Risk management, 29, 37, 65, 76, 78, 90, 110, 129
Lionel Robbins, 103
Christina Romer, 67
Paul Rose, 12-13
Murray Rothbard, 104
Nouriel Roubini, 73
Jean-Jacques Rousseau, 98, 101-102, 162
Royal Ahold, 30
Rule of 72, 24
Rule writing, 40, 50-51, 55, 56, 161-162, 166

S

Salomon Brothers, 27, 36
Sarbanes-Oxley Act/SOX, 21, 33, 57, 66, 71-72, 81, 87, 94, 102, 104, 106, 141, 148, 161
David Sarnoff, 5-6, 115
Savings & Loan/S&L, 21, 24-26, 44
Jean-Baptiste Say, 14
Say's Law of Markets, 14, 16
Myron Scholes, 27
Arthur Schopenhauer, 64
Joseph Schumpeter, 9, 18, 63, 136, 137
  Capitalism, Socialism, and Democracy, 136
Schumpeterian Economics, 17, 18, 28, 36
Scienter, 12-13
Securities Act of 1933, 115, 119
Securities Exchange Act of 1934, 39, 119, 151
Rule 10a-1, 39
Securities Exchange Commission/SEC, 21, 24, 33, 34, 35-37, 42, 51, 66, 69-70, 74, 82, 92, 105-106, 109-110, 111-112, 115, 116, 118
  Committee on Smaller Public Companies, 148
Enforcement Division, 35, 93, 94
Six Sigma, 85
Small- and medium-sized enterprises/SMEs, 50, 72, 118-120, 135, 137, 150
Small capital/cap, 12, 72, 109, 115, 126, 163
Adam Smith, 14
  The Wealth of Nations, 14
Social network, 5-7
Society for International Affairs, 3
George Soros, 10, 29, 35, 49, 63, 65, 157
Sovereign outsourcing, 148
Joseph Stiglitz, 16
SFO Magazine, 29, 35
Lawrence Summers, 60

T

Nassim Taleb, 99-100
  The Black Swan: The Impact of the Highly Improbable, 99-100
34-year bull market, 2-3, 6, 60
3Com, 6
Time Magazine, 5
Trend analysis, 29, 37
Troubled Asset Relief Program/TARP, 25, 44, 82
Tulip mania, 164
2008 subprime crash, 2, 4, 7, 8, 21, 22, 25, 35-39, 41, 56, 61-62, 66, 68, 74, 97, 100, 101, 105, 112, 123, 148, 154, 166

U

Ukraine, 88-89
Uncertainty, 12, 17, 39, 44-45, 51, 52, 55, 57, 61, 72, 73, 74, 78, 81, 87, 89, 91-93, 99-100
Unification, 122-123
United Kingdom,
U.S. Agency for International Development, 45
U.S. Census Bureau, 3
Private Securities Litigation Reform Act/PSLRA, 13
U.S. Treasury, 102, 104, 105, 116
  Financial Regulatory Reform, 65-88, 89-90, 102, 104, 112, 114, 160

V

Paul Volcker, 71

W

Wall Street, 9, 14, 22, 23-24, 41, 99, 161
Wall Street Journal, 91, 92, 146
Wal-Mart, 63, 108
Leon Walras, 18
Walrasian equilibrium, 18
The Washington Post, 130, 131
David Weild and Edward Kim, 117
Anthony Weiner, 57
Oliver E. Williamson, 108
   Transaction Cost Economics, 108
Wind trades, 165
Orville and Wilbur Wright, 55

Z

Zipf's law, 5